What the meaning of the book cover represents: The color aqua soothes our soul and creates an instant sense of home belonging to us. We are highly creative and discovered at a young age that we are gifted with many talents. Multiple talents are both a blessing and a curse because at times we may have difficulty choosing which one to focus on or pursue.

We have an eye for design and whether artistic endeavors, home décor, or fashion our innovative style and good taste shines in everything we touch.

People gravitate toward our warm and confident demeanor paving the way for us as a natural leader and communicator. We present a pulled-together vibe that attracts attention in all the right ways. Perceptive, intuitive, and sensitive—we are a good judge of character and can quickly size-up any situation.

The feather is a symbol of flight. It represents the ability to transcend and move beyond our mental barriers.

Ripples in water not only will heal those who we speak them over; they will accomplish that person's healing, then turn back like ripples in a pond and heal us, too.

How wonderfully he made us!

The song that goes along with our story of our lives is "God Only Knows" for King and Country

Our Journey and Healing
with God; Jesus; and the Holy Spirit

Our Journey and Healing
with God; Jesus; and the Holy Spirit

Lorna Goss and Jolene Rider

XULON PRESS

Xulon Press
2301 Lucien Way #415
Maitland, FL 32751
407.339.4217
www.xulonpress.com

© 2021 by Lorna Goss and Jolene Rider

All rights reserved solely by the author. The author guarantees all contents are original and do not infringe upon the legal rights of any other person or work. No part of this book may be reproduced in any form without the permission of the author.

Due to the changing nature of the Internet, if there are any web addresses, links, or URLs included in this manuscript, these may have been altered and may no longer be accessible. The views and opinions shared in this book belong solely to the author and do not necessarily reflect those of the publisher. The publisher therefore disclaims responsibility for the views or opinions expressed within the work.

Unless otherwise indicated, Scripture quotations taken from The Message (MSG). Copyright © 1993, 1994, 1995, 1996, 2000, 2001, 2002. Used by permission of NavPress Publishing Group. Used by permission. All rights reserved.

Paperback ISBN-13: 978-1-66282-267-4
Ebook ISBN-13: 978-1-66282-268-1

Dedication

Jolene's dedication's to my husband Steve He is my knight and shining armor he has helped me with myself confidence my ability to succeed he has been there and stood by me through the hardest trials of our lives together.

My daughter Jaime her gift to me is happiness self-esteem establishing faith. Our journeys together we have seen signs and wonders and miracles.

In Loving Memory of My Son Joshua Travis Dameron
I dedicate this book to my son Josh who passed away while I was writing this book he was so excited for me when I told him about writing a book about my life I know he's in his home in heaven cheering me on. His gifts to me is white rose's symbol of innocence purity and self-worth.

Lorna's dedication's my son Jacob his gift to me is to esteem. My daughter Delena her gift to me is gratitude and praise. I am so grateful for always having their support and encouragement.

Table of Contents

Chapter 1—Lorna and Jolene's childhood....................1

Chapter 2—Lorna's Story...............................35

Chapter 3—Jolene's Story 59

Conclusion... 123

No child should have to go through the childhood that we lived through. I do not even know how we survived. God had his hands on us since we were born to get us through what we had to go through. With what we had to endure, He had to have saved our lives many times because we were abused horribly in every situation, we were in. "A father to the fatherless, and a defender of widows; is God in his holy dwelling" (Ps. 68:5)

Lorna Jolene

Chapter 1

LORNA AND JOLENE'S CHILDHOOD

This story starts in 1956 in Portland, Oregon, the year Lorna was born. I was born three years later, in 1959. This is our story. We thank God that by his grace we are able to write this.

I was born prematurely and was not supposed to live. Our Mom had me at eight months. When she went into the bathroom, she saw that she had strings of blood coming out of her. When she went to lay back down, it felt like something broke when she turned over. It felt like hot water, but when the nurse looked under the sheet, she knew something was seriously wrong. They rushed Mom to the delivery room. They had to get me out in sixty seconds because I was drowning in the placenta—it was coming before me.

It just so happened that on that day, a specialist was there who knew how to save my life, and after my birth, I was put in an incubator for ten days. Lord says he who made you; who formed you in the womb; and who will help you: Do not be afraid" (Isa.

44:2). Mom was hemorrhaging, and she was in surgery for five hours after my birth. God had saved my Mom' life, Mom knew that God intervened that day. After we went home Mom could not do anything. She was bedridden, so she could not take care of me and had to have friend's come from her church to take care of me and the family.

When I was a child, I ended up in the hospital when I was a few months old with pneumonia. At that time, I was in a coma for ten days.

Lorna was five and I was three when our parents divorced, and our lives changed drastically. Because neither one of our parents really wanted us, they left us with numerous people who would abuse us severely.

A church our Mom was going to at that time told her that she was living in adultery with our Dad because they had been married before. She believed the church and divorced our Dad. This is the consequence of churches teaching the letter of the law instead of the spirit of the law when people believe them. "The thief does not come except to steal and to kill and to destroy. I have come that they may have life and that they may have it more abundantly" (John 10:10). "My grace is sufficient for you, for my power is made perfect in weakness" (2 Cor. 12:9).

That opened a door that should have never been opened; had been opened because of our Mom decision to divorce our Dad.

Lorna and Jolene's childhood

Caption: Dad Mom Lorna Jolene

We, as their children, had to survive the consequences of neglect and rejection and being severely abused by predators. When our parents divorced it made us feel unloved, unwanted, and abandoned. We remember feeling an aching loneliness and being physically sick. It also caused fear, confusion, and insecurities; and we felt unlovable and had a sense of never fitting in. Throughout our lives we had to deal with and overcome layers of trauma. We have gone through a lot of healing and have learned different prayers through the many mentors that God has brought to us to overcome everything we have gone through in our lives. And, all these things have led us here to these pages with the hope that we might be able to help even one person.

We moved to another town in Oregon with our Mom. After leaving our Dad, our Mom went crazy over men, She would be gone for hours and even days. I was left alone a lot with Lorna who, at only five years old, had to take care of me at such a young age. We know now that it was the Holy Spirit that gave her the ability and the gift of a mother's heart to take care of me and to prepare meals for us to eat. She remembers standing on the chair making Malt-O-Meal, and even though there were lumps in it, we ate it anyway.

It was a miracle that we didn't get hit by a vehicle when we went outside. Because the house was built by a sharp corner, the drivers coming from both directions would have not been able to see us. In Lorna's memories of that house, we were always alone there. Our neighbors next door had a dog kennel, and they gave us a German shepherd. They must have known we needed protection. The dog's name was David. Lorna remembers one time there was a knock on the door, and the dog was barking fiercely and wouldn't let us open the door. God used that dog to protect us. In many ways that dog was our angel.

Our Mom had a serious phobia of snakes, and Lorna's memory of the house was that the whole yard was full of snakes and snake skin. Our Dad would come over and kill them with a shovel. This is one of those memories that Lorna holds close to her heart; as it allowed time with just our Dad. In another memory Lorna had, she was at a park alone in an unsafe place, dancing and singing on top of a picnic table. A man showed up in a car and scared her so bad, she ran all the way home. What parent in their right mind would let a five-year-old go wandering off by herself to a park? This is how little love our Mom showed to us. On some level, I think that she was hoping we would just disappear.

The next memory we have was moving to the Oregon coast. Lorna was six, and I was four. Our Mom remarried, and her new husband was an alcoholic who sexually abused Lorna. Lorna found out later through a healing session that was the beginning of her eating disorder, in which she began gorging when she experienced triggers like boredom or frustration or any sort of anxiety. She would feel like she needed to punish herself with food or hunger, which this led to weight gain, and her poor self-image added more torment. No matter how much she bathed, she felt dirty, and she thought people could see her filth.

The next memory we have was after we moved in with our Dad. Our Dad left us alone a lot, and we had a lot of fear because He was not home with us all through the night. Keep in mind that Lorna was only five years old, and I was three. We were way too young to be left alone, even for a few minutes. We were so afraid in our Dad's house that we would pile up together behind the couch and sleep there. When we were behind the couch, we would be too scared to go down the hall where the bathroom was, so we would go to the bathroom in the kitchen garbage can.

One night we saw a man's boots through the bottom of the curtain through the window. We were so scared that we became paralyzed, and there was no one to reach out to for help. Another memory; we were home alone and it was getting dark; Dad wasn't home; we were out in the yard stricken in fear staring at our neighbors sitting in their home they must had seen the terror in our face's at our relief they invited us in and fed us potato chips. We don't remember how long we were there; but it was a welcoming break from the terror that we had known.

When I was a child living at our Dad's, I had a lot of bad nightmares, thinking that snakes were biting me. Our Dad had to put me in a bathtub in cool water to bring my high fever down and that relieved me from the screaming and crying.

Lorna and Jolene's childhood

Grandma Matilda

Our Grandma's home wasn't too far from our Dad's house. I remember one day when I was in her backyard while Grandma was attending to her garden. I was barefoot and got stung by a bee. I had an allergic reaction to it, and my body started swelling up and I had a hard time breathing; they had to rush me to the doctor. While I was there, they wanted to give me a shot. I was so frightened that I ran down the hall, screaming out of control. The nurse caught me and told me if I didn't get the shot, I would die, so I let her give me the shot.

Another time I remember when I was sick and our parents took me to the doctor. They wanted to give me a shot; I went out of control again, kicking my legs while lying on the table. The nurse was standing at the end of the table, and I accidently kicked her. After that, the nurse rolled me over her lap and gave me the shot. As a child I was sick a lot and as a result I received a lot of shots; I was terrified of them.

Lorna and I never got to experience childhood or experience school activities of any kind. We went to so many schools, we lost out on our education. We didn't get to spend enough time at school for Teachers to have time to notice that something just wasn't right. We were tossed around from place to place, and we remember that our parents were always putting us in harm's way by putting us with people who would abuse us horribly in unimaginable circumstances. They just didn't care.

One time, when we were in the care of one of my Dad's girlfriend's daughter, she would stick washcloths down our throats and try to choke us to death, and her son was always showing his naked body to us, trying to make us do sexual things to him. I remember one night when he was babysitting me, and he tried to get me to have sex with him. I tried sneaking on the phone to call my Grandmother, but he caught me and wouldn't let me have the phone.

I told our Dad about what he had done to me, and he got his gun and took me over to their house and had me confront him. The boy denied doing anything to me. It seemed to me that Dad took what the boy said as truth, but he never allowed for us to be alone with him again. Maybe he did do more than that. I just don't have memory of it. I like to hold on to that thought. That's the only time my Dad would have done anything to try to protect me. Lorna battled over the same things with that boy.

We were ages nine and six, and during this period of time, Mom's husband didn't want us around them. We hardly ever saw our Mom, but when she was around, she would stir the pot to bring in strife and try to turn us against one another. Lorna recalled one time she bought me a whole bunch of new clothes and didn't buy her any clothes. She was really hurt and crushed and shattered and rejected. Our Mom would use extreme competition to cause division between us by using mean words, and she made us feel unloved and unwanted, a burden to her. She is still trying these same tricks even all of these years later.

Lorna Jolene

Our Dad would also make us feel unloved and as if we created an irritation in his life. When we lived with him, he hired a babysitter who was so deep into her addiction to alcohol that she drank rubbing alcohol. She also smoked and would pass out with a cigarette in her hand that would fall to the floor and cause burn marks. Nothing was ever said or done about it. Between the cigarettes and the alcohol, it's a miracle the house didn't burn to the ground. But it was an easy solution for Dad; and he just allowed it to continue. In our memories of living with our Dad, we were always alone and afraid.

We have good memories at our Grandparents' house, and the times there were the only vacations that we ever knew. Our Grandma had a box of toys in the bedroom closet that we really loved playing with. It was an old farm set that included wagons and farm animals and a barn. We could create our own farm. We enjoyed sitting at the kitchen table with our Grandma. She had a drawer full of coloring books and games. She loved cooking, and she made us three full meals a day. The water was always cold and sweet tasting.

They had a barn with chickens and cows. We always had fresh milk and eggs, and Grandma would make her own butter out of the cream from the milk. She had her own garden, and our Grandfather raised bees, so we always had fresh honey. Lorna and I remember sitting outside with Grandma in the breezeway—that's what they did back then because there was no air conditioning—stringing the beans and snapping them. Grandma had a lot of picture albums of family and friends of hers that we didn't know, so she would sit with us and tell us all about them. These memories are the memories that we treasure the most. It was a carefree way to be kids and have some fun. It was a nice break from the terror of our home life.

Our Grandparents had a basement where we slept. There was a cellar down there, and Grandma would tell us stories about Raw Head and Bloody Bone's, so we were afraid to get out of bed in the middle of the night. It was Grandma's way of controlling us; if we stayed scared, we wouldn't get into stuff and stay out of trouble. It was cold down there, and it always felt like the sheets were damp. We always feared sleeping down there, and that was one of our worst memories when our Dad would take us there.

Even though we had some good memories, it was always around people or relatives who made us feel unloved, unwanted, and always a burden to them. Our Dad's family always had a sense of entitlement that they could treat us in a negative way. Our Dad never spoke up and protected us. We never felt safe and protected when we were with our Dad.

Lorna and Jolene's childhood

Granny and Grandpa Hale

The next place we remember, we were living with our Dad's sister and her family, where things were somewhat normal, other than our cousin who was hateful to us. There was a darkness in her. When she would take us swimming in the creek (there was no supervision with adults), she would hold our heads under water, and we thought that we would drowned. Even to this day we both still have phobia regarding water. Our aunt couldn't handle the stress, so we were sent back to our Mom and stepdad in Portland where we finished the last part of the school year.

We were always alone when in Mom's care, and a close family member began abusing Lorna; that continued until she was in seventh grade. One day, Lorna was sick with strep throat, and she was on the couch running a fever. A friend and I were lighting matches in the bedroom closet, taking turns locking the closet door and lighting matches. When I was locked in the closet, I set the closet on fire. I started screaming, and Lorna came and unlocked the closet door and got me out. We had to get the fire out, so we were running back and forth with pans of water in our attempt to put the fire out. Everything in the closet was destroyed. It's amazing to us that Lorna had sense enough to put the fire out. Once again the Holy Spirit had our backs.

After we finished school, we moved back in with our Dad who was wanting to find someone to take care of us because he had to work and had no one to help him. Our Mom had given him custody of us. She just gave us away without a thought, thinking we would be better off with him, but in reality, we weren't better off with either one of them. Our Dad answered a newspaper ad, and that's how we ended up in the care of our foster parents. This brings us to the next part of our story.

The year was 1966. Lorna was ten, and I was seven. Our Dad took us to live with the foster parents from the newspaper ad, but he really didn't know that would be when our nightmares of severe abuse would begin. They lived out in the country with no other houses around for miles, so nobody could hear our screams from the horrific and unimaginable abuse that was inflicted upon us. They had a small pond on their property, and when they wanted to punish us, they would take us out there and dunk our heads in the water. We were very frightened, which just added more fear of water.

They would put diapers on us made from bed sheets and made us sit on a toddler potty chair and suck on a bottle. It was very humiliating to us. We had to do all the housework because she was too lazy to do it. We felt like we were in a workhouse, being used as slaves and tortured. If there was a dirty dish after doing the dishes, she would make us do all the dishes in the house over again. We had to iron all the clothes for hours and hours. The clothes would be in bins in the front room, and one time we ironed for so long that Lorna's shoulder swelled up and she had to be taken to the doctor.

We were beaten every day with a belt. *I r*emember looking into a full-length mirror in the bathroom my body was full of black-and-blue bruises. One day, they made us beat each other.

We remember it was over one of their records that they said was missing, which was probably a lie. We said we didn't take it, but they said we would have to beat each other until one of us confessed. They made us beat each other with switches, and the bruises and welts would appear on our bodies when we were beating each other. Finally, we said that we took it even though we didn't so that we could stop the beatings. Because we told them that we did it, they isolated us from one another.

They did that a lot to us. We never got to play with each other like children do. We were controlled by fear and physical and mental abuse. We experienced defeat, and there was no way out. We were trapped. I remember one time when I didn't pick my clothes up off the floor, and they woke me up in the middle of the night and started beating me with a belt.

The next day the foster parents made me wear ripped clothes to school. I was very embarrassed and so humiliated that I went and hid in the bathroom and didn't want to come out. I don't know who it was that got me out of the bathroom; I'm guessing probably the principal. They took me into the office and started asking questions. Being frightened of what would happen to me, I can't remember what I told them. They did have the foster parent come and pick me up and take me to their house to change my clothes.

There was another time when they put Lorna in a back room of the house for her to sleep. She was scared so bad being back there by herself. They had put a heater back there, and when she awoke the heater was on the bed turned on. It had burned a hole in the bedspread. She was so scared she thought they were trying going to kill her.

There was another time that they gave me a little black puppy for my birthday. They had a ribbon around its neck. I was so happy, but soon they would use the puppy to hurt me. They took it away and never brought it back. It broke my heart. They gave Lorna a kitten that she loved and slept with and they did the same thing to her. She was so heartbroken.

Another time they made me stay home alone and sit on a bench in the hallway. It was at night, and I was very frightened. They told me if I moved off the bench, I would be in trouble. The foster parents said I did something wrong, that's why they left me alone. The abuse was so bad, we broke out in hives.

When our Dad would come and visit us, the foster parents would tell us not to say anything about how they were treating us, or they would threaten to beat us, so we said nothing. Lorna also remembers our foster parents had two children, a boy and a girl. The little girl wasn't even a year old; she was naked, using the couch to pull herself up, and Lorna saw her bottom all bruised up. Another time when our dad came to visit, he wanted to take Lorna somewhere with him. The foster mother told Lorna if she went with him, she would beat us so Lorna didn't go.

Lorna wrote a letter to our Dad telling him what was going on, and she put it under her bed. Our foster mother found it and beat Lorna. One day our Mom and her husband came to visit us, but they wouldn't let us see her—we had to stay upstairs. Our memories of the visit were of seeing our Mom sitting in the front room with our stepdad we was standing on the steps going up to our bedrooms, and Lorna remembers we were crying hysterically. When they left, we were running down the driveway, screaming for them to come back and take us home with them. They never came back to see us, and we were devastated, feeling trapped and alone.

When school was out, we went to live with our Mom and stepdad. The foster parents wanted us to come back and live with them again. After the summer, they told Lorna they wanted us to have our last name changed to theirs. They must have wanted to adopt us. They wanted Lorna to talk to our Dad about moving back with them, but she never did.

Living with our foster parents was a grievance of our minds, and we were shattered and traumatized.

When we moved back with our Mom and stepdad, we were in turmoil, screaming in terror. We had a lot of fear, and we couldn't sleep. We now know we had post-traumatic stress disorder.

Our Mom and stepdad were fighting and drinking all the time and hanging out at bars. We remember one day they came home fighting, and our Mom tried to kill our stepdad with a knife. We saw the whole thing. If it wasn't for a friend of our Mom who was there, she probably would have hurt him or killed him. The friend of our Mom pulled her off of our stepdad. We ended up moving in with that couple.

Lorna remembers that the day we moved in; the man started sexually harassing her. She fought that harassment the whole time that we lived there. We were always left alone. It was very seldom that there were adults around us. Lorna remembers us going to a park by ourselves with no supervision at all. I remember meeting a girl there at the park who wanted to hurt me. I was so afraid that I stayed in the house after that.

We both remember our Mom lying on the bed crying, the friend of our Mom's wife giving us pills to relax us. We don't remember how we survived being by ourselves all the time. After leaving there, our Mom went back to our stepdad, and we moved to another town in Oregon.

While living there we do have some good memories of going to school and getting involved in school activities. Lorna remembers excelling in arts, and she discovered at that time that she could draw. We also took accordion lessons. I was in Girl Scouts, and that's where I learned how to jump rope with two ropes. We made friendships, and we hung out a lot with our friends, doing kids things. We remember our Dad celebrating Christmas with us, which was very rare. We remember making taffy candy, with our Mom stretching the taffy. Those were good memories with our stepdad and our Mom.

We remember having pets there that we loved, and a tragedy with one of the dogs that happened when I was walking home from school. We lived by a busy freeway, and the dog was across the street. The dog saw me and came running across the busy freeway. A speeding car hit the dog, and I saw the whole thing. I was traumatized by watching that. Somehow somebody brought the dog in the house, and later it died.

There was still drinking and fighting going on there. One of the first fights there started in their bedroom. They were throwing ashtrays at each other, and there was blood everywhere. Our Mom was being beaten so badly that Lorna took a poker from the fireplace and hit our stepdad with it. We left the house and went to a phone booth and called the police. They came and arrested him, and the tragedy about the whole thing is our Mom got him out of jail the next day.

Our Mom left our stepdad, and we moved again close to downtown Portland. Our Mom got a job working in a bar, Lorna remembers she brought a biker home, who was in a gang. He stayed there with us; soon after he was there, he raped Lorna. It got so bad that our parents had to send her away to stay with family members in Montana. Our parents blamed Lorna for what happened to her, when our Mom was the one who brought the man home and allowed it to happen to her; the only way our parents dealt with it was to send her away without ever explaining or making it right for her. They made her feel she was the one who caused it. Our parents always put the blame on us when something tragic would happen in our lives.

I remember my cousin coming over and taking me to a party. They gave me a drug. After taking it, I was sitting on the couch and looking at the person across from me; all of a sudden I felt like I was floating across the room .I started screaming, so they sat me down on a chair at the dining room table to calm me down. Soon after that, my cousin took me back home to my apartment and left me alone. It was in the middle of the night, and everybody was sleeping. I was scared to wake them up. I went into the bathroom and looked at myself in the mirror, and my face looked like a skeleton. The drug must have been psychedelic. I was stricken with fear, thinking I was going to die. I went and laid down on the bed, frozen in fear.

While living there, we had some fun times. We would go roller skating at the rink. We would have to walk there with no adult supervision. It was a place we could go to get away from the dysfunction of how our lives were at home.

We were taken out of school and moved again. The next place that we lived with our Mom and stepdad was a beautiful place out in the country. This was the happiest time for us in our entire childhood. The farm had a barn, and there was a man who boarded his horses there. Our stepdad bought me one of the horses that the man owned, and the man taught me how to ride the horse. He would take me riding with him and his daughter. I would go out and ride my horse a lot. We had a big pasture for me to ride in, and sometimes the man and his daughter would take me riding in the mountains behind where we lived. They were very nice.

We had friends at school too. One of my friend's would have parties at her house. We would play games, and her mom would fix us food. We had so much fun. We had friends who lived next door. We would go out in the pasture and play baseball and play in the barn, all fun stuff that children do. I remember I had my first crush.

Lorna remembers fixing our Mom's wigs and her friends' hair. She realized at that time that she would like to do hair for a living. Her dream was to go to beauty school. She tried going after she had her first child but had to quit after three months because she couldn't find a babysitter. She tried to get our Mom to do it, but she refused.

All of that changed suddenly for us. Our stepdad and Mom were fighting a lot again, and they would have violent fights. We remember one time our stepdad brought home a gun and was going to kill us. Fortunately, there was someone there who knocked him in the bathtub and took his gun away from him.

Our stepdad was an alcoholic, and when he would come home after the bars would close, he would be so drunk that he let the farm animals into the house and cook in the middle of the night, around two o'clock. Our Mom and stepdad would always be fighting. They would wake us up when we had to go to school the next day.

We didn't have a washer or dryer, so Lorna washed all of the clothes on one of those old-fashioned scrub boards. She remembers her fingers bleeding. Our Mom and stepdad separated again. I lost my horse and the happy times that we had there as children came to an end.

It was another heartbreaking time for us. We moved into the small town in Oregon that was close to where we had lived on the farm. We moved into an apartment with our Mom. She wasn't happy having to raise us, and she started running around with men again. We were left alone again. One time Lorna was so sick she couldn't get out of bed. Our Mom happened to show up and got her some juice and soup and left again. She decided to go back to our stepdad, and that's when our lives took a horrible change. It was a bad nightmare that you couldn't wake up from. We were left with a neighbor we didn't even know. We were twelve and fourteen years old. She took us in, and soon we were into sex trafficking.

These are the six stages of grooming by sex offenders:

Stage 1: Targeting the victim. The offender targets a victim by sizing up the child's vulnerability—emotional neediness, isolation, and lower self-confidence. Children with less parental oversight are more desirable prey.

Stage2: Gaining the victim's trust. The sex offender gains trust by watching and gathering information about the child, getting to know his needs and how to fill them. In this regard, sex offenders mix effortlessly with responsible caretakers because they generate warm and calibrated attention. Only more awkward and overly personal attention or a gooey intrusiveness provokes the suspicion of parents. A suave sex offender is better disciplined and knows how to push and poke without revealing themselves. Think of the grooming sex offender on the prowl as akin to a spy—and just as stealthy.

Stage 3: Filling a need. Once the sex offender begins to fill the child's needs, that adult may assume noticeably more importance in the child's life and may become idealized. Gifts, extra attention, and affection may distinguish one adult in particular and should raise concern and greater vigilance.

Stage 4: Isolating the child. The grooming sex offender uses the developing special relationship with the child to create situations in which they are alone together. This isolation further reinforces a special connection. Babysitting, tutoring, coaching, and special trips all enable this isolation. A special relationship can be even more reinforced when an offender cultivates a sense in the child that he is loved or appreciated in a way that others—not even parents—can provide. Parents may unwittingly feed into this through their own appreciation for the unique relationship.

Stage 5: Sexualizing the relationship. At a stage of sufficient emotional dependence and trust, the offender progressively sexualizes the relationship. Desensitization occurs through talking, sharing pictures, even creating situations (like going swimming) in which both offender and victim are naked. At that point; the adult exploits a child's natural curiosity, using feelings of stimulation to advance the sexuality of the relationship. When teaching a child, the grooming sex offender has the opportunity to shape the child's sexual preferences and can manipulate what a child finds exciting and extend the relationship in this way. The child comes to see himself or herself as a more sexual being and to define the relationship with the offender in more sexual and special terms.

Stage 6: Maintaining control. Once the sex abuse is occurring, offenders commonly use secrecy and blame to maintain the child's continued participation and silence, particularly because the sexual activity may cause the child to withdraw from the relationship. Children in these entangled relationships—and by this stage they are entangled—confront threats to blame them, to end the relationship and withdraw the emotional and material needs the child associates with the relationship: whether it be the dirt bike the child gets to ride, the coaching the child receives, special outings, or other gifts. The child may feel that the loss of the relationship and the consequences of exposing it will humiliate and render them even more unwanted.

This is what happened with us. Lorna remembers the women standing on the front porch, watching us all the time. The women was nine months pregnant. Lorna's first memory was of the women when she started paying attention to her by bringing her into her home and putting wigs and makeup on her, making her feel special that someone would care enough about her to pay attention. Lorna enjoyed the attention because no one had ever made her feel that way. Soon after she had gotten Lorna's trust and got Lorna to thinking that she really cared about her, things changed quickly for the worse, and they began to groom her. That's when the sex trafficking began for her.

They were having her pose for pictures in different sexual poses and began to have her have sex with the both of them. My first trauma was when I opened their bedroom door and saw them having sex with her. I was so frightened that I shut the door and was paralyzed in horror. Soon after that it began to happen to me, they brought me into the bedroom, and her husband had oral sex with me. That was the first time anybody had done that. While he was doing oral sex with me, I experienced an orgasm. Later, when I left the room, I ran into the bathroom feeling confused, ashamed, and so frightened, not really knowing what happened to my body or why it felt the way it did. He didn't take my virginity at first, but soon after we were there, he did.

They manipulated and brainwashed us to join in orgies that they had in their apartment by using alcohol and drugs to the point we didn't know what was happening to us. I remember I told the women I didn't want to have sex with one of the men she had brought to her apartment. She assured me that I wouldn't have to, so I was so relieved. That night they had gotten me drunk, and the women let him take advantage of me anyway. The next morning when I woke up and realized what they had done, I went into the bathroom and was so traumatized by what had happened to me that I was sick to my stomach and felt dirty inside and deceived once again by them.

We felt like that a lot living in those circumstances, feeling so helpless we couldn't even hardly function. We had nobody to help us through it. We felt trapped and traumatized. Never experiencing fun, we were in a constant state of feeling like sex slaves, meeting everyone's needs but our own, and that was a very scary time for us. She would dress us up and put wigs and makeup on us to make us look older. She would take us to bars and put us in dangerous situations. She would give us drugs. She left me in a dangerous situation with some guy I didn't even know and took Lorna with her. I ran away from him and ended up in a bigger mess.

I was walking on the sidewalk when a guy stopped and asked if I wanted a ride. I was scared but got in his car anyway. He stopped at a store and bought some beer and asked me if I wanted one. I told him no. I had him take me back to the apartment where we were living. After I got there the man that picked me up asked me if he could have a kiss. I was scared but kissed him anyway. As far as I knew, he left, but what happened next is he probably stayed around there. I was there by myself in the apartment; and two men walked in, who I didn't know. They told me to go with them. I was scared, so I went. They took me to a bar, and when I was there, I saw the husband of the woman we were living with. I felt it must be a setup. I was so fearful and paralyzed. He didn't say anything to me, and he kept his distance, so I knew something was up. Later, the men took me to an apartment and drugged my drink, and several men raped me. I was in and out of consciousness. The next day they took me back to the apartment where we lived.

Looking back at how everything happened that night, I know now that the guy I ran from had it all set up with that guy picking me up. He must have told him to look for me. There must have been a lot of money involved. The women took Lorna away so that they could do that to me. With everything I went through that night, I know that God saved my life.

I was in sex trafficking for two years. I was fourteen years old when I got away from that lifestyle. Lorna got out of it sooner; she began to figure out what was going on. She knew she had to get out of there. She told me what she figured out and told me we had to get out of there, but I wouldn't go. They kept us separated and brainwashed, and I had so much fear that I didn't go with Lorna. Eventually I got out of there.

This is how. The women had dressed me up in a wig and makeup and took me to a bar. There was a guy in there whom I had met at a party with Lorna. I must have asked him to take me home with him because I left with him. I stayed with him at his house. When I left there, he took me to my Dad's.

After Lorna ran away, she was living on the street, sleeping on people's porches that she didn't know. A couple let her move in with them, and she babysat their children. That didn't last very long because the husband was making sexual advances toward her. Then she worked for some other people, and that didn't last very long because their house was haunted, and she was scared. She proceeded to live with several different families, and she was basically on her own. During the time we were in sex trafficking, our mom stayed friends with the woman who took us in. We would go and see our Mother, but we never did tell her what was happening to us; the woman must have told us not to tell.

When Lorna and I eventually were together again we were back living with our Mom and stepdad; we went back to school but only for a short time. One time I had a friend come over. We were alone in the house, and my friend was sleeping when I went into the kitchen to make myself some toast. I had burned it, but I started eating it anyway, and a piece of the toast got lodged in my throat. I was sitting down when it happened.

My friend was across from me, still sleeping, but I couldn't speak to wake her up. I started feeling dizzy, so I stood up, and while I was standing it felt like someone grabbed me and started doing the Heimlich maneuver. The piece of toast flew out of my mouth. Being a child, I didn't know then how angels can help you, but I know now that it was divine intervention that saved my life, not only that time, but many times throughout my life.

While living there, the woman who put us into sex trafficking would come over and take us to a clothing store and made us shoplift. She would bring big coats with her, and take us in the dressing room. She would put clothes on us and then she would put the coats on us to hide the clothing that we had taken to try on. During that time, I had met a friend at school, and we decided to run away. Being a child, I thought that was the answer to get away from what was happening to me, but it all fell back on me. During the time I ran away, one of the things I did to disguise myself was to dye my hair blonde, but it turned an orange-red color. We were caught and put in a juvenile jail.

It looked like a real jail with bars and the toilet, and shower were right where you had to sit. I had to stay in there for seven days. They blocked off where the beds were during the day, so we had to sit where the toilet and shower were. We had to do chores. I was so scared. After I got out of jail, I went back to live with our Mom and stepdad. Part of my punishment when I got home was that my stepdad made me go to school with my hair the color that it turned. The kids made fun of my hair.

Soon after that our Mom and stepdad separated. Lorna remembers when we left the house. She was in the house alone and saw our stepdad drive up to the house. She hurried and called our Mom who told her to hide behind the couch and that she would be there in a few minutes. Lorna stayed behind the couch until she arrived our Mom distracted our stepdad, so Lorna could get out of the house. Lorna ended up moving in with Mom's friend. That's when Lorna and I would separate again.

While we were living with our Mom, she brought over one of her girlfriends who had two sons with her. One of the sons started dating Lorna, and she moved in with his mother and eventually moved into a place with him. She lived with him for a year. Two major things happened to her during that time. She went to the movie theater and watched *The Exorcist* and ended up going twice with two different people, and that set off ten years of torment of fear, death, and phobias until a pastor's wife taught her how to fight her fears using Psalm 91.

The man Lorna was living with was addicted to drugs, and her life was miserable. She began taking drugs with him. That was one of the worst years of her life. She began by smoking marijuana, thinking that they would have something in common to do together, but it didn't change anything. Then she began to take cross tops, which is speed, and during that year she lost so much weight, she dropped down to seventy-nine pounds. One day, Lorna and her girlfriend went to the mall, and they thought it would be fun to go have their pictures taken in one of those picture booths. When she looked at the picture of herself, she was frozen in horror, seeing how thin she was. That was a real wake-up call for her. She knew she needed help. After he would leave for work, she would walk to a telephone booth every day and call family to come and get her, but they never did. Her way out; was when I was married for the first time.

I moved to another town with my Mom, and we lived in an apartment above a bar. That's where my mom went to work. While working there, she met a man and started dating him; later they would get married. They wanted to move to Nevada. I went with them on the trip to Nevada, and we stopped in Hood River, Oregon, the town that's famous for apples. We stopped there and picked apples in one of the orchards. We stayed in a cabin there, and we picked apples for a couple of weeks to make money for our trip and then left.

When we made it to the town where we were going, he got a job on a ranch. The people who owned the ranch let me and my Mom ride their horses, and that was fun. He taught me how to drive when we were there too. We were coming back from the town that was an hour away, and the road was straight all the way back to the ranch. He had me drive, but he wouldn't let me go over fifteen miles per hour. It took us a long time to get back there, but they probably didn't care because they were drinking. It was a really small town in the middle of nowhere. There was a bar and a post office. We would go to the bar and drink. I am surprised now that they let me drink in there. One time when the bartender was serving a drink to me, I was drinking 7&7. He said 7&7 make fourteen, so I knew he knew how old I was. They lied about my age; I was only fourteen.

We were drinking in the bar there one evening when my Mom and her fiancé got into a big fight. She left him there and took me and drove to the next town, which was about an hour away. She was drinking and driving. We stayed in a motel that night, and the next morning she went back and picked her fiancé up. Then we left, and we ended up back in Oregon.

I was still living with my Mom. I had turned fifteen. She and I got jobs at the same place. We were working at a laundry place. When I received my first paycheck, I wanted to go and buy some new clothes, and we went to one of the clothing stores. While I was there looking at clothes, there was a man in the store who kept staring at me and following me. He was with another woman. I didn't know that he had followed us home to see where we lived.

He must have taken the woman that was with him home, and he came back to where we lived. He started talking to my Mom's fiancé; he asked him if he could take me out. They said that he could, so we all went out to a bar. He asked them if he could take me with him by myself, and they said yes. He ended up having sex with me. He was a predator. He was twenty years older than me. He lied to us about a lot of stuff, and I later find out he was a womanizer and had several children. Much later I found out the woman he was with in the store was one of his girlfriends, though he told me that she was his sister. Soon after meeting him we would get married.

All the abuse and torment that we went through as children and into our adulthood caused us to have cycles of repetitiveness; always going back to the same kind of people who would abuse, torment, and reject us.

Our Journey and Healing

When Lorna and I think about all that we went through in our childhood; we realize how much God protected us. He gave us escapes in unimaginable situations; we never did get pregnant; we never got hooked on drugs or alcohol. He gave us his divine protection.

Chapter 2

Lorna story

At the time of Jolene's wedding, I found my escape. Our family members could see that I needed help. I was in a bad relationship, I had lost so much weight that I looked sick, so my family invited me to stay with them. I just turned eighteen, and the reality of what my Mom and Dad put me through was so painful; I felt like I couldn't tell my family. I began to drink because of the pain; I began isolating myself. I only left the house to go to work. This went on for about six month; when one day the Holy Spirit spoke to me and told me that my Parents were irregular, and He told me to make a choice—the choice was be happy or continue to be in the pain that I was in. I chose to be happy.

I didn't understand how to go about that so I decided to start going to the church that my Grandparents went to. There were a lot of young people my age there; here is what happened:

"During that time, after I was filled with the Holy Spirit, things changed; my surrounding felt like I was in the spiritual realm, and everything was clear. My mind felt more open, and it was like He lifted a load of darkness. I could hear God's voice clearer, and the Word of God became more alive. I poured myself into it and began to date a little. My new friends would come to church with me, and we were all involved with the church activities. It also involved the church in another town close by as well, and we had a great time together; we would take the snowmobile out with friends and enjoyed everything as young people do. That went on for months.

"Things began to change when a family member began to pressure me into dating the boy he went to school with; I was uncomfortable and felt a negative feeling about it. I was such a victim then I didn't know how to handle it so I didn't say anything. Then I was being pressured into marrying him; I didn't know how to say no so I fell under the pressure, and the negative consumed me. I didn't realize that I could go talk to someone. I didn't know how to communicate at that time. And, my excitement of my first love with God began to dim. Shortly after that the pastor and his wife were called to be evangelist. They left, and a new pastor came in. The church was still on fire and was full of people.

"My first husband asked me to marry him after that. I didn't want to I didn't know how to say no. I remember battling in my mind, feeling sick to my stomach; but I was so consumed with the pressure I said yes. I was working for the forest service, and I remember hiding my engagement ring not wanting anyone to know; on the day of my wedding I was getting ready at my Grandma house I felt sick to my stomach; holding back the tears I wanted so much to tell Dad to stop the wedding but he was always critical of me so I froze in fear and didn't say anything I went ahead and married him, and that's when the abuse and betrayal started again for me. Six months after the marriage, he began putting pressure on me to have a baby. All of our friends at that time were having babies, but I was making plans to go to beauty school. I ended up giving in and learned I was pregnant eight months into my marriage.

After that my husband started drinking and staying out all night, coming home drunk verbal abuse began; I felt trapped. Without any support or help from my family, I felt defeated and went into a deep depression .My pregnancy was very difficult, and I was uncomfortable most of the time. I ended up having my son a month early. I hemorrhaged and had an emergency C-section, my son's lung collapsed, and he had to be taken to another state because they didn't have the facilities to keep him alive. While my Mom and I were waiting for the ambulance to get there, the doctor and nurse had to keep giving my son mouth-to-mouth resuscitation, and I didn't get to see or hold him for nine days.

So many negative things happened at that time. My husband and I didn't have health insurance, and one evening my husband was on his motorcycle coming to the hospital, when a plywood board flew out of the back of a pickup and knocked him off of his motorcycle. After we brought our son home, my husband was so overwhelmed with the hospital bills and the responsibility of a baby, he tried killing himself. His Dad had to step in and help us.

My panic attacks started after I had my son. I remember one of the panic attacks that I had seems so hilarious now but it wasn't at the time. When I was having it, my husband was taking me to the emergency room. Our son was a year old at the time, and our pickup broke down on the way to the hospital. I began screaming that I was going to die, my husband got out of the pickup and flagged down a vehicle, which was a van filled with mentally challenged children. They put me in the front seat. My attack was so severe I lost control of my body; it was like I was having a seizure. When we got to the emergency room, they brought out a wheel chair, and my body was still out of control.

As they pushed me into the emergency room, the doctor laughed at me and told me that he was going to send me over to the mental health department. I was going to the emergency room on the average of twice a week. The doctor referred me to the mental health department and the doctor there told me the reason why I'm having these attacks was because I was breathing oxygen into deep; and that caused the carbon dioxide levels in my blood stream to drop too low. It would cause my heart to begin beating really fast, and that created symptom's like a heart attack. I felt like I was going to die. The doctor told me to carry around a sack, and when I felt like I was going to start to hyperventilate, I should breathe into the bag.

"Another thing that surfaced at that time was the eating and gorging would escalate. My weight was at a normal weight when it started. When I met this lady at church, we became good friends and shared our kids together. She was a beautiful lady and she had an hourglass figure. She was always concerned about how she needed to lose weight. That made me think that I needed to work on my weight, and that battle became a bondage. I suffered with this torment into my sixties.

"Jolene shared with me about a couple who had a healing ministry, and in my first session, I learned the root cause was when my stepdad abused me when I was six. God completely healed me in the first session."

After I had my daughter, the panic attacks progressively got worse, Because of the nightmares, I began to have fear of finding my daughter sexually abused, and believing that really happened to her, I got to the point where I didn't trust my husband around our daughter. I wouldn't let anyone babysit my children, including my husband, and would panic if anyone wanted to hold her. My stress was so bad the pastor's wife offered to babysit her, and I told her no. When the pastor's wife asked me why, I explained to her and told her that I was afraid that someone would sexually abuse my children. "I explained to her about my nightmares and the panic attacks, telling her I can't seem to overcome fear. She began to teach me how to battle against the spirit of fear and told me to read out loud Psalm 91. Then she told me to rebuke the spirit of fear; and read "God does not give us a spirit of fear; but power; love and a sound mind" (2 Tim. 1:7). She went on to explain to me from Matthew 18:18, 'Whatever you bind on earth will be bound in heaven; and whatever you loose on earth will be loosed in heaven.' That was my first lesson in spiritual warfare."

The pastor's wife found me a Christian counselor, and he told me that I was reliving the pain of my childhood through my children. The counselor told me to achieve something that I never achieved before but wanted to; I chose jogging. He told me to start out slow and choose small goals each day. He told me to walk to one telephone pole and jog to the next one, and that was my first achievement on the first day. He said it would make me feel good about myself and build my confidence. By using spiritual warfare, jogging, and learning to breathe right, it took me four years to overcome that battle. I jogged three miles every day through those four years I learned to lean on and trust in God.

Jacob and Delena

I began to see more in the spiritual realm, and God began to use me in intercession. I used the exercise to relieve my stress. When you are going through a panic attack, what your body experiences feels so real, you really believe you are going to die. I also learned to cope by getting involved with church activities, I surrounded myself with friends.

Another panic attack it was when my husband had to work swing shift. He had come home for lunch, and at that time I had a friend staying with us he was getting ready to go back to work and I panicked begging him to stay home. It was so bad I dropped to the floor and I grabbed his ankles. He pushed me away from him out of frustration because he had to go to work. After he left, I was so stricken with fear I became paralyzed. My friend asked me to smoke some marijuana with her, saying it would make me feel better.

I told her no, that it would kill me, she finally talked me into it, After smoking it I went and laid on my bed crossing my hands on my chest preparing for my death. Soon the marijuana kicked in and I got up and started dancing all over my living room telling my friend how normal I felt. I remember my friend was so startled when I came out of the room dancing, I could tell in her eyes that she knew I was nuts, I told her I hadn't felt this normal in a long time.

To this day Jolene and I both laugh when we share those memories together. I went through many more panic attacks throughout the years. The ones I wrote about we thought were the funniest. We still laugh about them to this day.

This was when I felt the first of the three shifts. The church was full, and the Holy Spirit was present for a short time; unfortunately that wouldn't last long. A witch started attending the church, and slowly there was a shift for the worse. My marriage began to fall apart even more. My husband started to drink heavily, staying out all night, only to return and beat me. I felt so trapped and isolated with no support and left with a feeling that I had no one to help me. I tried to reach out to the pastor and was told that the problem was me, that I needed to change and love my husband more.

One morning I was upstairs gathering clothes to dress my son, and my husband came up the stairs drunk. He hit me so hard that it knocked me unconscious. I was six months pregnant, and as a result of this beating, I lost my baby. I was so devastated when the doctor told me that he wanted my body to naturally pass the baby because I was at risk of a hemorrhage that would endanger me. The doctor gave me a D NC after carrying the deceased baby for a month, and I ended up hemorrhaging anyway. I remember feeling so physically weak from losing all of the blood that I couldn't even bring myself to hold my head up. As if that wasn't bad enough, my milk came in, this just added to the grieving.

I finally left my husband. I took my son and moved to another town and started the process of fulfilling my dream to attend beauty school. I couldn't find anyone to help me with childcare, so I would drive back and forth on the weekends because my husband found someone that was able to care for our son. I couldn't afford the living expenses, and I was struggling with leaving my son each week. So the pastor moved me back in with my husband. And on the way back the pastor told me that he wished that I was his wife and told me not to tell anyone. I felt so violated and traumatized. The next Sunday he resigned and left, which left me feeling like it was my fault.

The second shifting was when the next pastor arrived. The first thing that he wanted was to have the church give him money to build a new home; it was then that the evil started. He had a physical altercation with my uncle in a board meeting that took place at the church. The result of this act was that my family left the church. Many of the church members started to follow suit and left, one family at a time. The members of the church that had been filled with the Holy Spirit had been pushed out or disassociated. The church became what the Bible warns us to avoid, with jealousy, rage, hate, and resentment. The beatitudes were no longer present in what is supposed to be a Holy place of worship. The church leadership exhibited such an arrogance, and there was no longer love and acceptance there, only judgment.

One day, the pastor and the associate pastor, who I had known my entire life, came to my house. I offered for them to join me and my husband for lunch. The senior pastor accepted, but my friend did not as he was fasting. It was very evident that he was nervous and extremely uncomfortable. After lunch, the senior pastor sat in my living room and began to accuse me of something that I didn't do. My husband was furious. He made a stand, saying that he would no longer be attending that church. That was when everything began to dry up and die in my life. I continued to attend church because my friends went there, and it was an opportunity to socialize.

When my youngest child started school, I had a plan to save money and finally leave my husband. I found a job that provided me enough financial support to get my own place and leave with both of my children. I had so much hope of finally breaking free. I got out with my children, but it wouldn't come without a cost. My husband began to stalk me and beat me whenever he had the opportunity. This went on for several months. One evening I thought that he was out of town, so I went to his house to collect some of my belongings and I had my children with me. I opened the door only to find him there. He started yelling at me and begging me to return to him and be his wife.

He went to the bedroom and returned with a rifle in his hands. He pointed the gun at me and the children. I remember begging him to let us go. I promised him that I would come back just as soon as I dropped the kids off so that we could talk privately. He finally allowed me to leave with the children. I retreated to a good friend with whom I worked, who said she and her husband would help me. She phoned the police as soon as I arrived with my children. I was so grateful for her support and knowing that my children would be safe with them.

I was in such shock that I couldn't even think straight. I had been working the night shift and wasn't sleeping much. The police arrived and arrested my husband. After the arrest, my husband's Dad and sister had him committed to a mental health facility for evaluation. He was placed in the mental facility for several weeks, and that allowed me my first freedom in many years. Once he was out, I started struggling with my son. He begged and pleaded with me to be allowed to stay with his Dad.

I was so tired and was losing my ability to fight. So I ultimately gave in and allowed him to live with his father. This was one of my biggest mistakes and greatest regrets. I am grateful for my children's Grandparents who would take my son to their ranch to keep him safe whenever they knew that my husband was drinking. I am thankful for the protection and the memories that my son was able to build while being at the ranch. It was a safe place for him, and he still very much loves it even now as an adult. I was finally feeling free, but only for a moment.

My family, friends, and church members turned on me, telling me that I had made a mistake in leaving my husband. These are all people that had at one time or another taken me to the emergency room after a beating, people who had to hold my hand when, as a result of those beatings, I lost unborn children. My own Dad told me that I was stupid for leaving. There was no support. But I pushed forward and kept going through the process of filing for divorce. I moved away with my daughter, and we lived near my Mom for a time. Ultimately, we moved back to Oregon where I got a job working in the fruit-packing industry.

I found a church that also had a school for my daughter. I began to form a friendship with the pastor's wife. This was when the first start of my healing happened. I remember sharing with the pastor's wife about my family member who sexual abused me. She was the first person that I ever told this to. It was hard for me to even be able to speak, let alone form sentences, but she was so loving, kind, and patient with me. She didn't rush me. She just sat quietly while I tried to form the words. Once I was able to say everything out loud, she didn't speak, she simply wrapped me up in a warm embrace, and held me until my tears stopped. It was the first time in my life that I felt what can only be described as a mother's love.

It was the gentle feeling of being accepted as I am, with no judgment, only love. My healing journey continued; it was a very special time in my life. One day I was at her house, and the Holy Spirit drew me to a book that was sitting on her end table. It was titled *This Present Darkness,* a fictional Christian book about the spiritual realm. This was when I realized that there is a spiritual realm of angels and demons. I didn't know at the time, but God was preparing me for my next chapter.

After four years I returned to Wallowa County with my second husband; I was talking to Granny on the phone and making arrangements to stay with her until we could find our own place. No storage units were available, so she agreed to let us use her garage. Arriving there, I was shocked to see that my Grandma was in late-term Alzheimer's. Her dresses were burned in the back from keeping her woodstove open; she would stand in front of it to warm up. Her bed was full of feces; her body was dirty, and her dentures hadn't been cleaned for a long while. I was devastated that my aunt hadn't put her in a nursing home or hired someone to care for her. I talked to my aunt about her condition.

She asked me if I wanted to stay there and take care of her; I agreed. She told me later that she and my Dad talked, and they wanted me to have her home for taking care of her; I told her they didn't need to do that, but she wrote up a paper stating that I would inherit it. A few days later, they backed out of it. I took care of her about six months. One day they showed up and moved all her things, taking her to live with them, which lasted about a month before they put her in a care facility. They sold the place, and the new owners let us rent it; so it worked out.

The attacks started immediately. We noticed the bedroom we slept in kept getting colder, and we could see our breath. It didn't make sense; it was summer. I began to have a hard time sleeping at night. There was darkness in the room but didn't understand it. One night, I awoke to a dark presence. When I opened my eyes, I could see this movement. I was paralyzed, frozen. All of a sudden, it jumped on me and pressed me into the mattress, choking me. I couldn't scream or anything, and I remember thinking the name *Jesus, Jesus, Jesus*. Then it jumped on my husband, and he began to shake and tremble. He sat up and commanded it to leave, and it left. I told him about it the next morning, he didn't remember any of it.

Things just kept getting worse .My daughter began to get sick; she got so bad I had to take her out of school for two years and homeschool her. She ended up having her tonsils out, and she had a bad case of mono. During that time, she was in her bedroom, and I heard a blood-hurling scream. I ran in there and saw that her stuffed bear was talking and being thrown at her. We were both paralyzed.

I would sit on the floor at night in bewilderment, hearing deep voices, like the demons were talking to each other. I had so many sleepless nights. Another time, I just sat down from cleaning, and all of a sudden the dishes in the kitchen began to rattle. I don't remember how long I sat there frozen in horror. Soon after that, a family member came to visit. We were getting ready for bed and I opened my bedroom door to try and get it warmed up before retiring; and the ice-cold air came blowing in and hit us, gripping our bodies and causing our bodies to ache in pain.

That family member began to tell us of a time when he lived in an apartment. He said people there were practicing evil, and there was that same cold. One night, this demon pick him up and threw him against the wall. Another time, one woke him up by moving his foot. Then it clicked—spiritual realm, the book—I understood in a moment. What did I need to do?

One Wednesday night, I arrived at church late, and the lady speaker was new. She was talking about the spiritual realm. Later, at the end, she asked if anyone was experiencing anything like that to come up, and she would pray. I ran up to her and began to tell her what had been going on in our home. She and another lady agreed to come over the next day and show me how to bless my home. We began to go through the house, starting in the bedroom. She told me to anoint the doorway and the windows. She was praying when this demon hit the other lady and knocked her into the dresser and onto the floor. In a moment, the room returned to normal temperature; we moved on and went through the rest of the house. That was my second lesson in warfare.

The lady seemed to want to move in; she was at my house almost every day. At first, I felt grateful that God had sent me help, but the attacks seem to get worse. This went on for months. Then a lady that I knew from church earlier moved back and began to come over with words from God for me. Through her, God exposed the first lady to us; she was a witch. That explained all the attacks. It was like every day some sort of evil was showing up. It stopped after she was out of my life.

Lorna story

One Sunday night, the pastor ask the church to fast and pray and ask God to show us why the Holy Spirit had left the church. So I began fasting. God woke me up, and I was in an open vision. He was showing me what happened and why the Holy Spirit left. I understood then that there was witches in the church. This is the third shift. A few days later, The Holy Spirit told me to share with the pastor what He had shown me. He listened, but then he turned on me and said if God was going to tell anyone, it would only come through him.

After that things began to be more exposed. Friendships began to fall apart, and as a result of these changes, my very best friend broke my heart. This was a person I did everything with, confided in, and watched each other's children—everything that friends do. One day, when we were on a walk together, she told me that no longer would she be spending time with me because my husband and I didn't have a lot of money. Instead, she would be spending time with another couple. I went into a state of shock. I remember standing in my kitchen as my mind spun. I began to argue with myself—*there's no way she said that. Of course she did. You are not worthy of a friend*, and on and on this went on for days.

The person I trusted most turned her back on me. It was like going through a divorce but harder. Things just got worse in that church. There was repetitive rejection, control, a lack of love, and rigidity. The attitudes were condescending, critical, and destructive. Eventually, I was accused of heresy, and I left.

Our Journey and Healing

Lorna Jacob Delena

I began to heal up fifteen years later. I went to a retreat in Texas and have been on a journey ever since. I have learned so much, and I'm thankful for mentors and the experiences God has given me. When you think it's impossible, God always shows up to make the impossible possible. As I was getting ready to leave one of the retreats, I was talking to the minister and his wife. She asked me if I ever lost a baby or had a miscarriage. I said yes, and she said if I named them, I would get more healing.

I flew home that day; one of my friends stayed overnight and would go home the next day. Together we began to ask God to help me name my babies. All of a sudden I was in an open vision in which an angel came to me with the first baby. It was a boy—my daughters twin whom I had lost three months into my pregnancy. God named him Dan, and he came with the words jewels of righteousness and justice. The second baby was a girl whom God named Selena; she came with words of worth, safe place and snuggly. My third baby was a boy. God named him Jacob Isaac Peter; he came with the words jewels and heart. The fourth baby was a boy. God named him Aarohan Henry and he came with a sword and purity. The fifth was a boy whom God named Gallahan for kingship; he came with a bowl of Jesus's blood. My sixth baby was a boy; God named him James Isaac, and he came with purity and shield. The seventh baby was a girl; God named her Monica Flower. She came with the words moneyed and radiant with jewels. My eighth and final baby was a boy; God named him Gallahan Bruno; he came with the words grace and pardon. I was blown away and received so much healing from grief and sorrow. I felt so much joy! I was so surprised I had so many miscarriages; I had them between my son and daughter.

I always longed to have a relationship with my Dad growing up. He would always reject me and abandon me whenever I would try to be close to him. I was deeply hurt in most of my childhood and adulthood until one day the Holy Spirit told me to call him so he could hear my voice. I was so angry with God, remembering all the times my Dad rejected me. I was so upset about it that I talked to my husband. He gave me the greatest advice; he told me to be the best daughter I could be and do it for myself so when he passes away I won't have any guilt or regrets. I called him, and I could tell in his voice that he was really touched, so I began a journey with my dad. He told me he was sorry for rejecting us as children, and he told me that he put other women over us. The love of God came through our Dad and ignited a great journey of adventure. We went on many train rides, watched old movies together, and laughed and cried together. He had a great personality. I realized during that time that we should never give up on our dreams. I'm so thankful to have had one year, enjoying my time with my Dad. It was so awesome to experience the love of my Dad I can't wait to see him again.

Lorna Dad Jolene

I'm feeling naked, sharing things of my past that I had stuffed and never really talked about, feeling unworthy, embarrassed, and crying out to God for help. And He gave me this word from John 15:16:

> Ye have not chosen Me; but I have chosen you; and ordained you; that ye should go and bring forth fruit; and that your fruit should remain: that whatsoever ye shall ask of the Father in my name; He may give it to you.

He went on to say:

> You are chosen by Me. Why do you say, "Lord, choose someone else?" I have chosen you and ordained you and placed you in me and I will be glorified in your life. I choose the foolish things to confound the wise and the weak things to confound the mighty. I choose what others have thrown out, pushed aside, and said there is no way. I will do what others thought was impossible for you, in you and through you.
>
> I have plans to prosper you and give you hope and a bright future. I will free my power in you and

use you to set many people free. I will awaken your spiritual senses and use you to awaken and revive many. You know what it is to be empty. Now you will know what it is to be completely full. You know what it is to be naked and afraid, but now you will know what it is to be clothed by me. You know what it is to live in fear; now you will know what it is to live by faith. I have chosen you to live, move, and have your being in Me.

Don't say, "Lord; choose someone else." My choosing is right, and My ways are perfect. I have chosen you for such a time as this. You will show my love and power to a world that is hungry for me. You will align yourself with My will and trust My choosing, and I will increase you more and more. I will cause great grace to abound toward you. I will meet your every need, and I will direct your every move.

So much is waiting for you. I have many things to show you. I have many things to give you; but I am waiting for you to accept that I have chosen you.

I accepted it, and I'm blown away.
Two weeks later...

Waking up into an open vision; I was looking up at my babies; they were jumping up and down and cheering me on; in that moment I knew they were my eight babies I lost in miscarriages. I was so overwhelmed by their excitement and love for me; as I was watching them I was taken higher up to eye level; at that moment my earthly Dad moved into the vision; moving in close with the babies he was young and the glory and brilliance and colors in his complexion was indescribable; in that moment I understood you would only see that in heaven. He smiled with such joy and happiness that overwhelmed me I felt so happy and overjoyed for him that he is so loved by the Father in heaven. The atmosphere was overwhelming love from the Father. Then I was taken higher to the Father in heaven he then drew closer to me and he put into me the words I was given two weeks before it was like they grew into me with the Father and we became one at that moment I was undone I felt the atmosphere of love penetrating my soul and on the outside it was swarming around me. It's so exciting to serve God and have a close relationship with him every day there's a new adventure!!!

Chapter 3
JOLENE'S STORY

I was fifteen the first time I got married. I felt pressure from the dysfunctional lifestyle, living with Mom and her fiancé, knowing that they really didn't want me there. My mom believed his lies and thought he had a lot of money. This man was the one who stalked me all the way home. When I think about it now, it was another way that Mom got rid of me. Because of the pressure my Mom put on me to engage in this unwanted marriage, I went ahead and married him.

We were married in a church close to where my Dad lived. My Dad bought me my wedding dress, and it was beautiful. My family came to our wedding, but none of his family came. I had never met any of his family. Later I would find out that one of my husband's girlfriends lived close to my Dad. She had two of my husband's children. He was a bigamist, and our marriage was another example of my parents getting rid of me at any cost.

Our Journey and Healing

Jolene Mom Lorna

We really didn't have a honeymoon. We just got a motel room close to where my dad lived. We ended up living with my Dad, and I'm thankful for that. Who knows where I would have ended up; when three months into the marriage I got pregnant? He wasn't home a lot because he was with the other women who had his children. They would call me and tell me that he was there. After they would call me, I was devastated and didn't want to believe them, being so young and naïve.

My Mom and Dad had made a terrible mistake, and I was trapped again in another situation. I left him. I had nowhere else to go, so I went back to my Mom's house. While I was there, my husband called my Mom and wanted me back, so she sent me back with him. He took me to Texas while I was pregnant. We lived in a small town, and while I was there with him, I found some pictures of him getting married to someone else. I asked him about the pictures, but he tried to tell me it was something else they were doing. He must have thought I was stupid.

One time he came home, and he came up to me and put his arms around me. I didn't see the gun in his hand until he put his arm down. He must have wanted to kill me, but something must have stopped him. When I look back at it, I know God intervened and took care of me that day. After that, I was so frightened that I wanted to leave. He had one of his friend's take me back to Oregon.

We drove back in his friend's car. Oregon is where my husband's friend lived with his family. It was a long trip from Texas to Oregon. I was eight months along in my pregnancy, but he tried to molest me several times. I was very scared being in the car with him all that time. I couldn't believe that he would want to have sex with me being pregnant. I didn't even know him. I know it must have been God protecting me that made him stop. He took me back to my Mom.

After I left my husband, I gave birth to my son. We were living with my Mom and her fiancé. She was tired of us living there, so she took me over to where her sister lived. I didn't know at the time about her plans to go over there and just drop us off in an apartment that she rented for us. She just left me and my son there. I was only sixteen, and I didn't know anything about raising a baby. I was scared. I had no vehicle. I started seeing a guy that knew my aunt. He treated me well. He bought me clothes and things for my son, but I really wasn't happy with him.

Lorna found out what my Mom had done to me, and she and my cousin moved me out of that place. I know now that it was God who used them to get me out of there. I went back and lived with my Mom again because I didn't have anywhere else to go. When my husband called and wanted us back again, I didn't want to go back, but my Mom convinced me to go.

I flew back to Texas where he was living in another small town, and there was another woman hanging around him there. I didn't stay for very long. I hated it there; it wasn't a good place for me and my son. My husband flew us back to Oregon to live with my Dad. I don't know how my Mom found out that I was back, but she showed up at my Dad's house. She was with her fiancé and his son. I had met his son before I went back to Texas. They wanted me to go back and stay with them so I went.

I decided not to go back to my husband, and soon after that we divorced. I started dating my Mom fiancé's son. I didn't feel that I had any other choice. Considering the way my Mom was always trying to get rid of me, who knows where I would had ended up if I hadn't. I had a miscarriage after divorcing my husband.

The past year, Lorna had told me about her miscarriages and God taking her into the open vision and naming her children. I knew that I had a miscarriage early in my pregnancy and asked Lorna to pray with me to see if the baby was a boy or a girl. It ended up being a boy *and* a girl. Lorna ask me if I wanted to name them; I was so overwhelmed with excitement to know that I would have had twins, I really couldn't think of any names. She told me to ask Father God to name them, and He did.

Here are the names He gave them and their gifts to me. He named the boy Christopher Lee Alan. Christopher means Carrier of Christ, and his gift to me is strength. Lee means God is my judge, and Alan means: Harmony, stone, noble, fair, and handsome. He named the girl Sophia Maria, Sophia means wisdom or wise; her gift to me is precious purity, and innocence. Maria means beloved. It was such a healing to me for my babies to have names and to know what a loving Father we have. He cares and loves us so much.

After I got with my fiancé, later we would get married my life changed. With the lives that Lorna and I had lived, we missed out on having a childhood, getting an education, going to proms, and just being normal children and teenagers. We missed out on so much. A short while after we began dating, my fiancé wanted me to start studying with Jehovah's Witnesses

My fiancé was raised Jehovah Witness, and he wanted me to start studying with them. I didn't know anything about the Holy Spirit at that time and how He lives inside you. I had a bad experience when I was a young child; when my mom took us to a certain church, so I never felt comfortable with the Holy Spirit. The experience made me feel scared.

When I went to one of the Jehovah Witnesses' meetings, everything was calm and quiet. They don't believe in the Holy Spirit living inside you. I didn't know anything about the Holy Spirit and the Trinity. The Jehovah's Witnesses don't believe in the Trinity.

I thought I felt comfortable there, but the way they treated us wasn't good. My fiancé had an addiction to alcohol and gambling, but instead of helping him or trying to find help for him, they ended up disassociating him. In that organization, if you have problems with addiction or family problems and you are baptized, instead of helping you spiritually through the Bible, they disassociate you and you can't have any other contact with them unless you change to the way that they believe.

We weren't really accepted there, but they scare you so bad about reading other churches' literature or other Christian books or going to another church. They tell you that other religions are false, and that you will die forever and not be resurrected. They keep you scared. We stayed in that religion for ten years because we were afraid to go to another church. We experienced a lot of bad situations in the Jehovah Witness religion.

When my son was around nine months old, I had my first anxiety attack. We were living in an apartment, and we only had one vehicle. My fiancé was at work with the car, and I was home alone with my son. I was seventeen years old and scared. When I woke up that morning, I felt like I couldn't breathe. I felt like I was going to die. I ran to the neighbor's house to use their phone and called a taxi to take me to the hospital. I took my son with me because I had no one to babysit him.

When I was seen in the emergency room, the doctor told me I was having an anxiety attack and that I just needed to calm down. I really didn't know what he was talking about. I had never heard about anything like that before. He never talked to me about what was happening to me or why my body was feeling like it was.

I left there feeling defeated. I called a taxi to take me and my son back home. On the way home, I was telling the taxi driver what I was going through with my anxiety attacks. While I was talking to him, I noticed the meter and realized that I didn't have enough money to pay him to take us all the way home. I told him that he would have to let me and my son off so that we could walk the rest of the way, but he just turned the meter off and took us home. I didn't know how the Holy Spirit worked back then, but I know now that he had sent the right person to pick us up and help us through our situation.

I didn't get the help that I needed. Doctors didn't know how to treat anxiety attacks back then. I went through many years having them and feeling like I was going to die any minute. Later I learned from Lorna that her doctor had told her she was living her childhood pain through her children. I know now that's what happened to me.

I was a young mother having my first child when I was sixteen, and the pain of my childhood surfaced in me. I had a lot of fear of people hurting my children through the years. I had a real struggle with disciplining my children or letting their dad discipline them. Any kind of discipline seemed abusive to me. As a result, my husband and I would fight continuously about how to discipline our children. Through the years, the fear was so real to me that I started having panic attacks. They were so bad at times that I would go to the doctor's or to the emergency room on a weekly basis. I constantly feared that I was going to die. Nobody understood what I was going through, not even the doctors.

At that time, I started going to church for help, but all I got there was more fear, stress, and condemnation. My eating disorder surfaced at this time. I would starve myself. I was afraid that someone would poison my food. I had to smell my food before I would eat it, or I would serve the food to my husband first to see if he would have any reaction to it before I would eat the food myself. Eating became a torment to me. When I did eat something, I would put my finger down my throat and make myself vomit. I went through that torment until I was in my forties.

When my healing began, I didn't know anything about getting healed from my past abuse. At that time, I did not know how many years of healing I would have to go through to overcome the pain of my childhood and the anxiety attacks it caused. My anxiety attacks started in 1970 and lasted into the mid-1980s.

After a while, my family and I decided to move to the town where Lorna lives. My Mom and her fiancé followed, Month's later mom got married; at that time Lorna and I learned that we were both pregnant. I went into labor four days after Lorna had her son. We had our babies in the same hospital. Lorna was still a patient there when I went in.

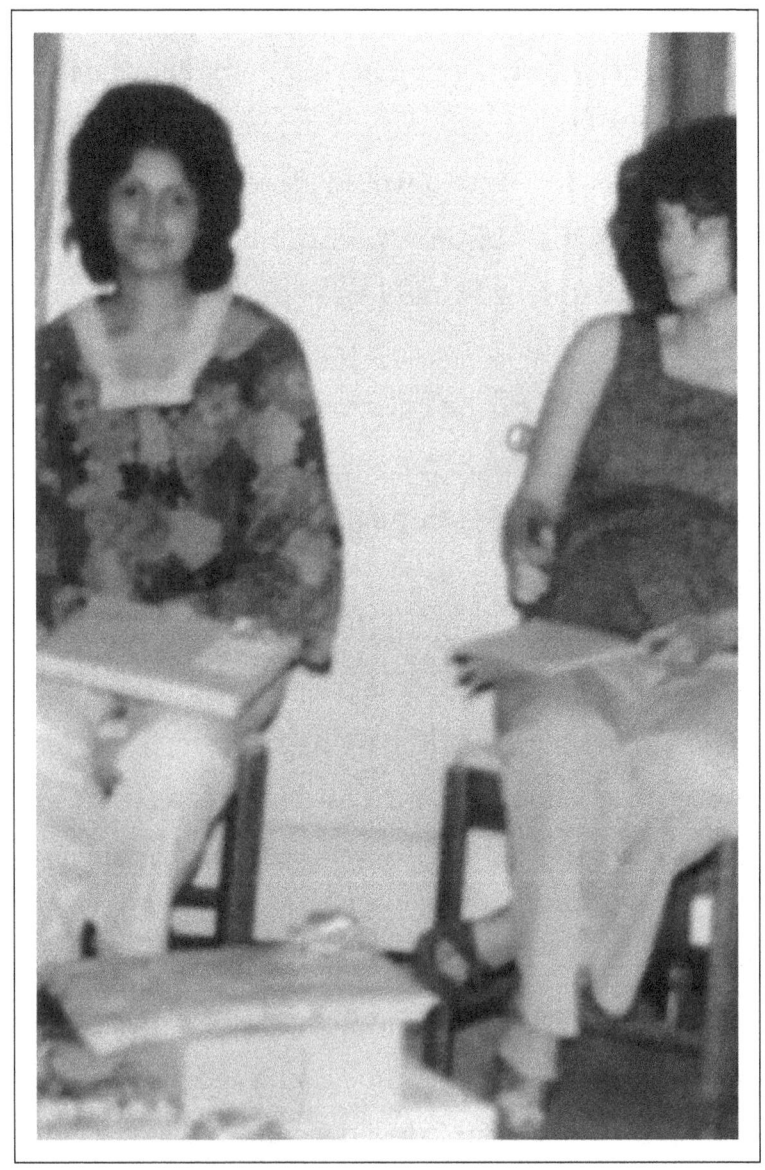

Jolene's baby shower with Lorna

Jolene's Story

They induced my labor because I was two weeks overdue with my daughter. Inducing my labor caused me to have a hard delivery. They had to go up inside of me to turn my daughter. I wanted to have her naturally, so they didn't give me anything for the pain. When that happened, you could hear me screaming loudly. I had arched my back up off the table. Lorna and Mom were watching the whole thing happen, but they ran out of the room because it was horrible for them to watch. After I gave birth, the doctor showed my husband the placenta where it was torn, and they told him that was the reason for the birth being so difficult.

> We couldn't find work in Oregon, and we were struggling financially. So we decided to move to Nevada. We found work there; I went to work in a fast-food place. While working there, the manager sexually harassed me. One day when no one else was there, he cornered me, and he tried to kiss me. I was so scared I never went back to work there after that happened.

I went to work in another restaurant where I had another anxiety attack. I went to cash out a customer, and all of a sudden, I felt like I couldn't breathe and felt like I was going to die. I ran back in the kitchen area and called my husband. He came to pick me up; and took me to the emergency room where, once again, I was told I was having an anxiety attack and was told to go home and drink a glass of wine. I still didn't know what was happening with my body.

I started going to a church there. One of the women tried to get me to receive salvation, but at the time I was scared, so I stopped going to church. Soon after that incident, we left and moved back to Oregon.

Two years later, I gave birth to another son. We were living around my husband's sister and her family. We were celebrating Halloween with her when I went into labor. My son was born Halloween night. After my son was born, we were again struggling financially. My Mom and father-in-law were living in another small town in Nevada. They told us that we could find work there, so we moved back to Nevada with them where we were able to get jobs. My Mom trained me to be a waitress, and we worked at the same place. We made good tips, and with my husband's job, we were able to make a living.

I left Nevada after fourteen years and moved to Oregon close to where Lorna lives while living there I went to get some counseling; I talked to the counselor about how it was in the foster home and how it had affected my life. The counselor thought that it would be a good idea if I went back to the house that we were abused in. The counselor told me to take someone I trusted. Lorna and I didn't live too far apart then—about an hour from each other. I asked Lorna if she wanted to go, and she said yes.

Lorna Jolene

The place was about four hours away from where we lived, so we took that trip together. When we got to the big hill, where the house was located, we both got such a sick feeling in our stomach's that we didn't think we could go through with this idea of going back to revisit the site of such a nightmare from our past. We stopped and prayed to God that we would have the courage to do it and that He would come with us.

When we got there, nobody was home, and we were able to get out of the car. Everything looked the same, but the pond that they would dunk our heads in was a lot smaller than we remembered. When you're a child, everything looks bigger to you than it actually is. The house looked exactly the same, even the land looked the same. We went through a lot of healing together on that trip, and we know that God had planned us to go back there in His timing. Everything went according to what He wanted us to do with nobody being there. We didn't even know if they still lived there. The Holy Spirit protected us again.

My husband could not get control of his drinking problem, and after eighteen years, I left him. My children were teenagers at the time, and we moved to Arizona for about a year. Then we moved back to Nevada and I began to waitress again. In December of 1999, I met the man that I would eventually marry, and we are still married. We met at the restaurant where I was working at that time. He was new in town, having moved there from Texas, and he would come in and eat there all the time. My

Mom worked at another restaurant, and he would go in there and talk to her sometimes. I had changed jobs during that time and didn't tell him where I was going to work, but since it was a small town, it was easy for him to track me down, and he started coming in there. I was working on one of the days that my Mom came in, and he was in there also. We all started talking, and he asked me if I would like to go with him to another town, which was an hour a half away. I told him I would only go if my Mom could go with us. He said okay so we went. We had a good time together, and we have been together ever since. That's when my journey of healing from my past was about to begin, It's been an intense journey and has gone on for years.

We stayed in that town for about a year. My fiancé had gotten another job in another small town that was about an hour from where we lived, so we moved over there. My children and grandchildren moved over there also. They had their own places. My daughter Jaime and son Josh and I worked in the same restaurant as waitresses and waiter. While we were living there, my daughter found out that she had Hodgkin's lymphoma. It was 2001 when she learned her cancer was in stage two.

When we first found out she had cancer, I put a contribution box up on the counter for help with expenses. One night my daughter and I were working, and I didn't see the older gentlemen following me to the back of the restaurant where we picked our food up. I must have felt somebody following me because I turned around and saw him. My daughter was beside us, and the gentlemen told us that he would know the day that my daughter was healed of cancer. At that time, I didn't know that God uses people to give you words of hope and healing. I know now that the gentleman in the restaurant that night was our angel. We've never seen him again.. We had to take her to the closest big city which was four hours away. We found a really good doctor there who took her insurance, and that's where she went to have her chemo and radiation done. We drove back and forth from where we lived for her chemo treatments. When she had her radiation treatments, we stayed close to the big city in our RV trailer for a month. In 2007; my daughter was diagnosed with thyroid cancer from radiation treatments she'd received from her Hodgkin's disease. She survived that; and she has been cancer free ever since. She is a survivor.

Soon after being healed from her cancer, my daughter and grandchildren moved to Oregon, and my son moved to Missouri with his fiancé's family. I went to Oregon to be by Lorna while my fiancé went back to Texas. This would be another journey of my healing. Lorna has been a Christian since she was eighteen. The only church I went to in my adulthood was the Jehovah Witnesses, so I knew nothing about salvation and asking Jesus into your heart. She asked me if I wanted to do that, and I said yes. While I was there, we were going through some healing from our past, and I was having some bad experiences. You should not go through healing unless you are with someone who knows how to help you through it.

Jaime

There wasn't anyone there who could help me spiritually with everything I was going through, so I called my daughter and asked her if she wanted to come and see me with her children. She said yes, and when she got there, she could see I was having a hard time. About that time, my fiancé showed up and moved my trailer to the town that was an hour from where I was staying in Oregon. My daughter stayed with me while he went back to Texas.

It was while I was living in that town that I met some people who prayed with me, and on August 2, 2003, I was saved and filled with the Holy Spirit. With the problems that I endured with Lorna praying for my healing from my past, it was just too much. At that time, she didn't know how to pray for deliverance from the demonic forces like she does now. When things started surfacing, God led me to these people who knew how to pray.

It was a very special time for me. They explained what had happened to me and spent a lot of time sharing scriptures from the Bible and explaining them to me. After we were done, they took me to town and bought me a Bible of my own. We attended a church there, and the church was going to pay our way to a women's retreat—they even had a babysitter for my daughter's children—but we had to leave suddenly, and we didn't get to go. We went back to Nevada. My daughter and grandchildren went with me because they didn't want to stay in Oregon.

When we got back to Nevada, I went back to work at the restaurant where I had met my fiancé. I worked there a short time before my son called and wanted us to move to Missouri. He flew to Nevada and helped us drive back with him. He drove the U-Haul, and we traveled in my car behind him. That was a long drive. When we first got into the town where we were going to live, my daughter saw a church on the side of the road and said we should go and check it out. This started another journey with our walk with God as a family.

While attending that church, my children and grandchildren and my son's fiancé and her sister all got saved and filled with the Holy Spirit. We were all baptized there. At the time, my son had injured his back and had back surgery, so he got baptized after us on another day. The pastor was so impressed because he got baptized so soon after having back surgery. What a glorious time that was. The church was going to have a women's conference in Branson, Missouri, and the pastor told my daughter that she and I would need five hundred dollars to go. I had been working at a restaurant as a waitress, but right before we knew about the conference, I had quit my job so my daughter and I didn't have much money and neither did my fiancé. My daughter had some money that we were going to use to go to the conference, but we had to spend some of it. We decided that we were not going to go because we didn't have enough time to get the money we needed, but God had a plan for us.

On the day before the conference, we were driving around with my son's fiancé. We wanted to go get something to eat. My daughter and my son's fiancé wanted to go eat at a Mexican restaurant, but I told them that the Holy Spirit wanted us to go to the place where I just quit not too long ago. I was hesitant about going but went anyway. When we walked in, we saw our pastor and his wife eating at one of the tables. They invited us to eat with them, so we did. While we were sitting there eating, the pastor asked us if we were going to the women's conference. We said no because we didn't have enough money. The pastor told us that it was a divine appointment for us that we go. He said that he was going to pay our way and to go get our nails done and get whatever we needed for the trip with the money we had left.

My son and his fiancé watched my daughter's children, so she could go. It was definitely a divine appointment for us. At the second session of the meeting, I had an awesome experience with the Holy Spirit. They started singing the song "Jesus Loves Me," and I could hear Jesus say to me that He could remember me singing that song to Him when I was a little girl. I broke down crying and the women from our church came over and started praying for me. One of the women singing in the group on stage came down to me and told me that God had given her a scripture that morning to read to someone there, and that someone was me. The scripture was Romans 9:21. In the Message Bible it reads:

> I'll call nobodies and make them somebodies; I call the unloved and make them beloved. In the place

where they yelled out, "You're nobody!" they're calling you "God's living children."

I didn't know who she was, and she didn't know who I was. I was so amazed that she was able to know how that verse was just how my life was growing up and that's how people, including our parents, we were around made us feel.

After the morning session was over, we broke for lunch. They told us to sit with people we didn't know so we could get acquainted with other women. A couple of women came and sat with us, and one of the women started talking about what a bad childhood she had and how God had helped her and the close relationship that she had with Jesus. I was sitting there thinking how I would love to have a relationship like that with Jesus. I told them about one of the men at our church who told me that God put it in his heart to give me a journal. I had no idea why God wanted me to have it, so I asked them what I should do with it. They told me the reason God wanted me to have it was because He wanted me to start writing down things that had happened to me and my most intimate thoughts so that I could build a relationship with Him.

After the women's conference I started doing that. We went to workshops after lunch. My daughter and I were drawn to the same workshop on how to go into your own business. My daughter was asking God what she was supposed to do. God gave her a vision of a place where women who have cancer could go and have a babysitter for their children and get pampered with beauty treatments.

> "In the Last Days," God says, "I will pour out my spirit on every kind of people: Your sons will prophesy, also your daughters; your young men will see visions, your old men dream dreams. When the time comes, I'll pour out my Spirit On those who serve me, men and women both, and they'll prophesy. (Acts 2:17)

The next day was the last day of the assembly, and that was another awesome day for me. The woman who was the speaker said at the end of her talk that she had a word from God for one of the women at the conference. She was looking straight at me. I looked behind me to see if someone was sitting there, but there was no one. She said I have a word, and the word is for the beautiful woman sitting right there, and she pointed to where I was sitting. I was just amazed that she would have a word for me. I had no idea why God chose me, but He told me I always wanted to do something for Him someday and my someday is now.

When I left there, I thought what He told me would happen right away. I didn't know that He wanted me to go through so much healing over the years that followed. When the session was over, the woman who read me the scripture in the second session came over to me and told me Jesus wanted her to give me a ring so that every time I looked at it I would know that I was a jewel in His eye. Now how awesome is that? She also gave me a copy of The Message Bible. I still have the ring and the Bible, and they are very special to me because Jesus thought that much about me to give them to me.

The pastor was right. It definitely was a divine appointment for us, and we are so thankful to him for paying our way. That was the first assembly we ever attended where we could really see and feel how the Holy Spirit works. It was the greatest experience. Thank you, Jesus for letting us go. My daughter and I started attending that church in the summer of 2004, and we were all baptized in December of 2004. God started healing my broken heart, and while attending that church, I also was healed of a hiatal hernia.

One day I met a very good friend there who the Holy Spirit told to write down words for me that He wanted me to have. She wrote them for me in obedience to Him. Those words that the Holy Spirit gave me have been with me ever since. Everything that He told her to write down has come to pass over the years. They did not happen right away. It has taken years, but most of the words He wrote me have been fulfilled through my journey with Him.

I will always treasure the time I got to spend with my son. He passed away in May of 2018. February 2006 is when I left Missouri with my fiancé and went to Texas. Before I left Missouri, I had forgiven my Mom for things that had happened in my life. We stayed in a lot of motel rooms in the beginning. When we first went back there, my fiancé worked during the day, and I was left alone in the motel rooms. I didn't have a car then; I had left my car in Missouri with my daughter.

Being by myself so much of the time, the Holy Spirit started healing my body. I would lie in bed, and He would do healing's on different parts of my body. I really don't know everything that He was doing. He started healing my teeth. I never experienced anything like that before. As a new Christian, I didn't know what was happening to me. It was like I was at a dentist getting my teeth worked on. The Holy Spirit worked on all of them, but I didn't feel any pain. It was like someone was in the room with me, using dental instruments.

Looking back now, I know it must have been angels and the miracle of God what He did for me in the beginning of my journey of forgiving my Mom amazes me. I went through a lot of healing in those motel rooms. I will always cherish that time with him of experiencing supernatural miracles.

Soon after that when we rented an apartment while Lorna was living in Oregon. She called me and told me about a healing retreat that she went to in Texas. She thought that it would be good for me to go. One of her girlfriend's sisters knew one of the ministers who had gone there and who lived close to where I lived. I called them to see if they could take me with them on one of the retreats, and they did. They were the kindest people.

Jolene Dad Lorna

When the session started, they asked who would like to be prayed for. After watching the people there get prayed for, they looked happy and not scared, and the woman I was with ask me if I wanted to get prayed for. When I said yes, peace came over me like I never felt before. It was such an awesome experience. They served us breakfast, lunch, and dinner there. They always prayed over the food, and the food tasted really good. It was like it was anointed.

When I got back home, my fiancé was working a lot of hours, and I was left alone a lot. Shortly after I got back, I took a plane trip to Lorna's house again. She didn't have a bedroom for me to stay in, so I stayed with one of her friends. While I was in Oregon, my Dad's caregiver passed away in the trailer that they lived in, so I went to the part of Oregon where he lived. When I was there, he didn't look like he was doing very well, so I asked him if he wanted me to stay there with him. He said yes, so I did.

After I was there a while, I saw that a renowned minister was having one of her conferences close to where my Dad lived. I really wanted to go, but didn't want to go alone; I called Lorna and she couldn't go; but she had a friend who did. My Dad and I went up to where Lorna lived. I wanted to get my hair colored while I was up there. On the day I made the appointment, I didn't know my Dad wanted to go back home. When I found that out, I was already getting my hair done. He wanted to leave right then. He didn't wait for me and left me there. I stayed with another one of Lorna's friend's.

It was around the time when the conference was going to start so I went to it with the friend of Lorna's who wanted to go with me. My fiancé paid for my half of the trip and my half of the motel room. We hardly knew each other, but we had a good time when we were at the conference. At one of the meetings, the special speaker said that she was going to do something the Holy Spirit wanted her to do. She said I'm coming out of my comfort zone. She said everyone there was going to get their heavenly language. When I received mine, it was so awesome! I could feel the Holy Spirit come upon me. It was such a powerful experience.

After the conference, Lorna's friend took me back to my Dad's house. I stayed there with him for a few months, and we spent a lot of time together. He liked watching a renowned minister on television. He said he really liked listening to the minister's uplifting messages. I would pray for my Dad, and I asked him if he wanted to invite Jesus into his heart. He said yes, so I said the prayer with him. I know that the Holy Spirit healed him from the things of his past.

One time when I was praying for him, the Holy Spirit touched him, and he fell back while sitting on his couch. I waited there, holding his hand, until he came out of it. He just seemed so much happier. He lived in a gated community for seniors, where the residents would all get together to eat meals and play games. I got to be friends with one of his friends, and we would do a lot of things together with my Dad. My Dad's granddaughter called and told my Dad that my half-sister had suffered a stroke. She lived in the state of Washington not too far from where my dad lived. A friend of my Dad's took us over there to see her. Before we went, I had called Lorna to pray for her. I had a book with prayers in it, and one of the prayers was the prayer to receive salvation. The Holy Spirit prompted me to bring this book with me.

When we got there, we went in to see her. I was sitting on a chair close to her bed. I was scared and hesitant to ask her the questions I knew the Holy Spirit wanted me to ask her. I had never been really close to her. She was one of the first family members I led to salvation other than my Dad, so I was pretty nervous and didn't really know what to say. My Dad said that he wanted to leave, so I knew it was now or never.

I sat by her. She was sitting up, and I asked her if she wanted to ask Jesus into her heart. She said yes, so I let her read the prayer in the book I had brought with me. Then I prayed for her healing. Later I found out that she recovered, and I knew that God gave me that time with my Dad for her to get healed.

I didn't have my Dad in my life too much as a child, but I will always cherish the time we got to spend together then. I remember like it was yesterday how he loved trains and how we went to this park where there were running trains that you could ride. My Dad and I rode on them together. His friend went with us and took pictures. When I think of the memories of my Dad, this is the time in my life with him that I cherish. Our Dad made it right for Lorna and me at the end of his life.

When I was at Lorna house, she reminded me about the healing retreat I went to when I was in Texas. She said they were having another one that she thought would be a good one for us to go to for more healing. I called my fiancé when I was there visiting her and asked him if he would pay for our way there. He said that he would, so while I was staying with my Dad, we made reservations to go. Lorna came down to where my Dad lived to meet me, and we took our flight from there to Texas.

I started going through some weird stuff at my Dad's house and at the retreat as well. While I was staying there, demons started having sex with me. I didn't tell anyone what I had gone through, not even Lorna. We were getting ready to return to Oregon when the next day, one of the ministers' wives came to pray with us. While we were praying, she told me that I needed to stay there and get more healing. I did, and Lorna went back home. I really didn't know why the minister's wife wanted me to stay there. I still hadn't told them what I experienced at my Dad's house before I went there. I wish now that I had. I may not have had to go through what I went through there if I had told them.

Lorna Jolene

I didn't know at the time that Lorna had been interceding for our bloodline for years. Now we understand that God was preparing us for ministry. When I was at the retreat, I went through a lot of scary things. I was hallucinating and not understanding what was going on with me. I was there during the time that there wasn't a healing retreat. I was staying in the dorm by myself, and that's when the demons again started having sex with me. I would meet up with one of the ministers during the day, and sometimes at night he would take me into town. We would pray together at the church and talk about things that I was going through, but I never did tell him about the molestation of the demons.

They had another retreat while I was staying there. Other women came and stayed in the dorm with me. At one of the meetings, another one of the ministers wanted me to tell about what I had gone through growing up. I know the Holy Spirit gave me the words that He wanted me to tell. My testimony touched a lot of the women and blessed them. One of the women there had a rash on her face, and when we went back to the dorm, they came looking for me so I could lay hands on her for her healing. Another woman who was staying in my room with me told me that she felt me put my hands on her and pray for her healing. She told me that she was healed. Even though I was going through hard things, the Holy Spirit showed up for me and used me for other women in need when I was there.

Jolene at retreat

I went back to my Dad's house, and I started seeing a nutritionist. Lorna started going to her also, and she did some things with our bodies to help us with more healing from our past. She was the first person who told me that I would write a book, but she didn't tell me what it would be about. With the Holy Spirit's help, I found a pastor at a church not far from my Dad's house. My Dad would take me over there, and the pastor would talk and pray with me in the sanctuary; and that began a season of healing through crying the time that I spent with him. When Lorna was there, he would pray with her as well. After I was back at my Dad's I started hallucinating and going through a very hard time. Lorna lived five hours away from my Dad. My Dad had called her and told her what I was doing, so she drove to Dad's house. When Lorna got there, they took me to a mental institution.

While I was in there, I went through some pretty scary things, again hallucinating and reliving the things that happened to me in my past. I stayed in there for two weeks. This all happened in 2006. In January of 2019, I went to a healing session and found out more about why I went through those scary things. My Dad's caregiver had died in their trailer before I got there. When I decided to stay there with my Dad, the demons that were on her manifested on me, and that's why I was going through scary things at my Dad's house and at the healing retreat that I had attended. In another healing session I would get my answer of why the demons were able to assault me. I wasn't healed at the time I was staying with my Dad. The demons were able to have access to me and molest me. I know it wasn't a nightmare. It really happened to me. I have since met women who suffered similar experiences; and they too were victims of early molestation and sex abuse.

I was mentally unstable from years of abuse from my childhood. I had never experienced anything like that before. You can see that it took many years to find out what really happened to me. I am so thankful to God that I finally had gotten my answer and that I wasn't crazy. I realize that we have to cover ourselves with God's protection every day through reading the Bible and learning how to do warfare. Lorna and I have learned how to do warfare, and through the years God has brought many prayers to us through the people and pastor's that He has brought into our lives.

Soon after I got out of the mental institution, my fiancé wanted to come to Oregon and get married. When I was at the healing retreat, God told me that he had chosen my fiancé for me. While I was seeing the nutritionist, I told her that I was going to get married. This was in the month of September, and she told me to get married on the tenth because the number 9 means letting go of the past and the number 10 means new beginnings. So that's the day that we picked. I called Lorna and asked her to pray with me that God would guide and direct us to the right person to marry us.

Lorna searched the internet and found the right minister. She called her, and she said that she would marry us. My Dad lived close to the Oregon coast, and that's where the minister that Lorna had found lived. My Dad and his friend took me to find my wedding dress. I bought some colored sand so when we got married, we could blend the sand together, and I bought some wine glasses and a bouquet so that we could make a toast to each other. We were all set to get married.

Steve and Jolene

My fiancé flew in from Texas. My Dad let us use his car, and before we left for the coast, I got my hair and nails done. On the way there, we stopped, and I picked up a little cake. When we got there, we went to our motel room and got ready, and then we went and met with the women who was going to marry us. It was really cold that day on the beach, but we got married anyway. We didn't have anyone to stand up for us, and there weren't very many people on the beach that day. While we were walking along the beach to find the perfect spot to get married, a couple of people came up and started talking to us. We asked them if they would like to stand up for us, and they said that they would.

We had forgotten our camera in the room. Another woman came up to us and told us that she had a camera in her room, so we waited for her to go get it. It was a long walk back to her room, but she was willing to walk back there and get it. She took pictures of the wedding, and after the ceremony, we gave her our address. Soon after we got home, she had sent us the pictures. The women who married us had written the vows for our service. They were beautiful, and she gave us a copy of them before we left. I had written words to my fiancé that the Holy Spirit helped me with. It was a beautiful ceremony.

After we were married, we went back to the woman's place who'd married us. She had a little reception for us, with cutting the cake and toasting our love for each other with the wine glasses. She took pictures of the reception. I know that God was there with us that day, putting everything in divine order for us. After our honeymoon, I went back and stayed with my Dad for a little while longer. I treasure those days that I got to spend with him now. I wasn't able to see him again before he died. He passed away on January 13, 2008.

Steve and Jolene

I went to Texas to live with my husband, and while I was there, I started hallucinating and going through some hard stuff again. It was like a nightmare to me, again going through the same stuff that I had experienced at my Dad's house and at the healing retreat. My husband couldn't find anybody to help him with me, but through the grace of God we survived that time together.

I had another breakdown. This time, my husband took me to an emergency room, and the doctor there put me on some medication that helped me get better. My husband found me a psychiatrist, and she's been helping me ever since. I haven't had another breakdown since then. That was another one of the darkest moments in my life, but the Holy Spirit still used me to help people.

He had me write words to people. He even used a part of the words from our vows. I started sharing them over the phone with some of the people and the pastor and his wife in the church I had gone to in Missouri. After some time, I wasn't sharing them, but God had another perfect time for me to start sharing them again. It would be years later.

While I was living in Texas, I started having major problems with my stomach, and I went to a couple of doctors there. They ran some tests and one of the doctors told me that I had gastro paresis, saying there was no cure for it. After that, I found a nutritionist who was also an MD. He helped me some, but my stomach still felt the same. I went to another nutritionist MD in Nevada; who cured me of chronic fatigue syndrome years earlier; and he thought that he could cure me of the diagnosis that I received Texas. I got some relief, but my stomach felt the same.

I left there about a month later and went back to Texas, still not being able to find a cure for my stomach. My husband got a new job in another town. My stomach wasn't getting any better, so I looked online for a nutritionist near where I was living. I started going to see her in 2013. I started cleansing my body and getting colonics. It worked for me for a while, and then I got really sick. The only things I could eat were watermelon and peas. My nutritionist could see I wasn't getting any better, so she had my husband and I move into a little cottage on her property. She started me on the Gerson diet. That's where you drink fresh vegetables from a juicer and eat healthier. I was still getting colonics right along with the diet. The nutritionist thought that it would take me a month to get well, but one month turned into six months, and I still wasn't getting any better.

We needed to find someone to take care of me because we couldn't continue living there. I called Lorna and told her we needed to start praying for God to help us find the right person to take care of me. She prayed that God would handpick the right person. It was soon afterward that the nutritionist who was taking care of me wanted something done in her house. One of her friends new a guy who does work on people's homes, He brought his brother with him; and he would be the answer to our prayer. His brother and his wife just had moved up here from Indiana, where his wife worked at the Mayo Clinic. They had only been in Texas for two months when they came over to the nutritionist's house to see what she needed done. She was so desperate to find someone to take care of me that she was asking everyone if they knew of somebody.

She asked them if they knew of anybody, and the brother told her that his wife would know how to take care of me since she had cooked at the Mayo Clinic, so he gave her their phone number. They never did come back to do the work that she wanted them to do. That was another divine appointment that God had planned for my life. Soon after the man was there, his wife called about the job to take care of me. My husband hired her; she took care of me for four years. She took me to all my doctors' appointments, made my juices, and cooked my meals. I could only eat organic vegetables and potatoes, but it had to be mashed up like baby food. I wasn't able to eat any meat or fish at all or any other kinds of food. She stood by me through the good times and bad. She was my angel, and we knew God sent her to me.

After leaving the cottage, I was still getting colonics every day and doing home enemas. I was still doing the Gerson diet, but I still wasn't improving. My husband started looking for another doctor for me. He had his secretary on the phone all day long, every day, looking for a doctor who could help me. Many of the places she called were not taking new patients, and my husband was getting to the point of giving up. That's when he asked God where He wanted him to take me. A doctor's name came up on his computer, and his office was only an hour away. He is an MD nutritionist and a Christian doctor. He told my husband that they pray for their patients for their healing. After everything that I have been through, I had lost all faith in God. I didn't understand why He wasn't healing me after everything that I had gone through. We decided to go ahead and go anyway. They needed us to sign a paper that it would be okay for them to pray for me, so we signed the paper.

Jolene's caretaker Ysneida

The doctor helped me to start eating regular food; my caretaker didn't have to mash it up anymore and soon I was able to start eating meat and fish and other kinds of food. I was able to stop getting the colonics and was able to go to the bathroom on my own again—and he helped me to regain my trust in God. He explained to me that I was like an onion that had to be healed in layers and that it would be too much for me to handle if God healed me all at once. He told me that I didn't only need physical healing but spiritual healing, and he explained how important it was to be healed together to get complete healing. He prayed for me at all my office visits. He also had his prayer partners pray for me every Friday. They also prayed with my caretaker. She received a lot of healing too, and she and I grew together spiritually. She is such a loving person, and she would do anything for you. We have a unique friendship because we went through a lot of things together. We are more like family.

My prayer partners helped me to have faith and to begin to trust God again. The Holy Spirit began to lead me to share the words he put on my heart with others. One morning I woke up, and I was thinking about a hamburger place where my husband and I had eaten before. It was Fuddruckers; I was wondering if there was one in this area.

I had forgotten about it until one day when my caretaker and I had gone to my doctor. After seeing him, we decided we wanted to get something to eat. We couldn't get across the freeway to the place we wanted to go, so I remembered wanting to eat at Fuddruckers. We drove a little way down the road and saw a sign for Fuddruckers, so we went there. When we got there, there was a waitress, and it was like she was waiting for us. When we went into the restaurant, she started giving us words from the Holy Spirit. I realized that our decision to stop for lunch there was a divine appointment for us.

After that, we stopped there often. Soon the Holy Spirit wanted me to give her words. When the appointed day arrived, I told my caretaker that it was the day the Holy Spirit wanted me to give them to her. My caretaker's daughter went with us. When we got to the restaurant, the waitress started telling us that she had been asking God questions, like how He feels about her and what He wanted her to do. I had brought the words with me and told her that this was her answer from God.

It is such a blessing that God touches everyone. When we gather together, we were all touched, and my caretaker's daughter saw for the first time the hand of God touching each one of us. She was so amazed.

I started going to another healing place close to where I live. When they pray for you there, they ask Jesus into the session. When they were praying for me, I received healing words from Jesus about the things I went through in my childhood and adulthood. I'm still not completely healed, and I'm still going through spiritual healing for my past. The doctor was right when he told me that I am like an onion, and God has to heal me in layers.

It's been the same for Lorna. She has gone through years of healing throughout the years, and she is still not completely healed up either. In 2016, I got a call asking if I would go pick my granddaughter up.

She was seven years old at the time. I thought that I would only have her for a short time, and I took a plane to Las Vegas to pick her up. I made the flight there and we came back the same day.

When I arrived home with my granddaughter, the Holy Spirit woke me up one morning. He reminded me of the words He gave me when I was in Missouri. They said "I have chosen you, my child, to do the job I have assigned to you. My grace is sufficient for you. How must I work in one if that one has never been tainted? I have been with you all along—you say it seems forever. It is this that I am trusting in your care." The words the Holy Spirit gave me go on to say more, but that is the part He wanted me to hear because it was about my granddaughter. At the time He gave me those words she wasn't even born. Nevertheless, we ended up adopting her.

My caretaker helped me take care of her until I was well enough to do it on my own; and my husband also took on the responsibility of her care. He has been there for her. She didn't know anything about God, Jesus, and the Holy Spirit. We started teaching her about them. My prayer partners also prayed for her when I went to my doctor. She received salvation on April 3, 2015, with a prayer partner. She wanted to get baptized, so I asked one of the pastor's if he would baptize her. He said he would, so we set the date for the weekend of her birthday.

I didn't know at the time we set the date that my daughter would be visiting us with my grandson around that time.

Jolene's Story

Jaime Jolene The grandchildren are around the same age—eight months apart.

I asked my grandson if he wanted to get baptized, and he said yes. We decided that they would be baptized together, and we made plans for them to be baptized in a pond at a park close to where we live. The Holy Spirit wanted me to play a song called "Flawless" by Mercy Me before they got baptized. Everyone that attended the baptism stood around in a big circle, and we prayed and played the song. I was standing with my daughter and my caretaker. My grandchildren were across from us, and when the song started playing, the children came over to us.

Jaime Jolene Ysneida Brandon Haley

We gathered in a circle, hugging each other. I know that the Holy Spirit was doing some healing to all of us then. It was a very emotional time. Afterward, we walked over to the pond in which they were going to get baptized. A lot of people we didn't know were gathered around the pond with their children. They were there watching the baptism. The pastor baptized both children.

Haley

Brandon

After he baptized them, he knew that the Holy Spirit wanted him to ask the people if anyone else would like to be baptized. Seven other children were baptized that day—our God is so awesome. A couple years later when I went to the healing center, I got the words from Jesus about the baptism of my grandchildren, and these are the words: "God is writing his story through you. You have already witnessed a harvest of souls seven times greater than you could have imagined when you planned your grandchildren's baptism."

My daughter and I started attending a church after she'd been here about a year or so. In May of 2018, my youngest son, Joshua Travis Dameron, went missing. He left his home on May 12. He was only supposed to be gone for a couple of hours, but he never returned. That was the last day I talked to him. I was able to tell him that I loved him. It was the day before Mother's Day. He would always call me or text me to tell me, "Happy Mother's Day."

Jolene Joshua

I never heard from him that day, so the next day I called him he didn't answer his phone; so I called his dad and he said I haven't heard from him. He told me our son had left the day before he was worried because normally our son would usually call him to let him know where he was. After two or three days, his dad called the cops, and told them that our son was missing, but they said it was too soon to put out a missing person report.

Several days went by without hearing anything from Joshua. My daughter put the kind of car he had, a Mustang, and what he looked like on Facebook. She didn't hear anything for a couple of weeks. We were praying for answers and desperate to know where he was.

We learned about a person who had seen Joshua's car out in the desert for a week or so. Curious, he finally went over and checked the car out. He found a receipt from an oil change that Josh had in the glove compartment and put it on Facebook. The person was messaging my daughter; that he found the car, and he wanted to know who owned it he said "Did anyone lose a car?" My daughter messaged him back and told him it was her brother's car. The police didn't do very much to find him. If it wasn't for my daughter putting his car and his picture on Facebook, we probably wouldn't have had closure to this day.

After we found out where the car was, my son's dad called the police and told them the car was found. They performed a search for his body. The first time they searched, they had to stop because there was a tourist attraction going on at the Hoover Dam. The next day they went searching again and found his body a mile and a half from where his car was found.

Because it had taken so long to find his body, his remains were unidentifiable. We had to get his dental records to identify him. When Josh had been missing for about a month, a prayer partner and I started praying and speaking in tongues together on the phone that he would be found.

Josh's body was found soon after we got done praying; that was a miracle. I believe that our praying in our prayer language reached God, and He answered our prayers. I was expecting that Josh had passed away. I was hoping that he would have been found alive, but his body was found in the desert; it had lain in the hot desert sun for a month. He was found on June 16, on my grandson's birthday. We know that he died in May, but because they couldn't identify the precise time period that he died, they had to put down the day he was found and was pronounced dead.

I am so thankful that God left enough evidence to be able to match him up to his dental records. I felt in my heart that God protected that evidence so that our family could have closure. That was my worst nightmare: knowing that my son had died such a horrible death. There are no words that can describe the way I felt. The only thing that has kept me going is my belief in God and knowing that my son is in heaven with Him, living out his destiny and dreams.

Josh

A few months before his death Josh was drawing closer to God. He went to a church in Phoenix, Arizona. He was so excited to tell me what happened to him the first time he went there. The reading and discussion that day was on the prodigal son, and the pastor called Josh out of the audience and brought him on stage. The pastor was telling him words from God. Josh was crying when the pastor was telling him those words. I remember he was so excited that happened to him, and I am so thankful that he had that experience before he passed away.

Knowing that God would do that for us and give us such a wonderful memory when Josh was still missing gives me something special to hold on to. My daughter and I decided to go over to one of my prayer partner's house to pray for Josh. On our way over there, we saw a Mustang that looked a lot like Josh's car stopped at a stop sign. When we drove past it, the light was red. We stopped at the next light, and while we were stopped the Mustang that we saw pulled right next to us. It was like God was trying to tell us something about Josh.

When we got to her house, we started praying. God told me that Josh was in heaven with Him, and my daughter saw two visions of Josh in the back seat of his car, curled up in pain. There were two people in the front seat of his car, and the driver was driving really fast.

> I will pour out my spirit on every kind of people.
> Your sons will prophesy also your daughters your
> old men will dream your young men will see visions.
> I'll even pour out my spirit on the servants, men
> and women both. (Joel 12:28)

We didn't say anything to each other about what we had seen or heard that day until we found out what happened to Josh. We were probably too traumatized to think that could be true, so we didn't say anything about those visions.

The way Josh was found we know that he was murdered. The police didn't do any investigation because the guy who found the car searched the car, and the police said that he sabotaged the evidence. They chose not to do any investigation and closed the case. His death certificate says the cause of death is undetermined. Ever since my daughter and I saw that Mustang, no matter where we go, we see them. We could be clear out in the country and still see them. God has comforted us by showing us Mustangs. Josh really loved his car, and it has really been comforting to us to see them wherever we go.

You never know what God is going to do to comfort you through your loss of a loved one. The church that we go gave Josh a beautiful celebration of life. My sister's daughter helped us out so much; she put together a slide show of Josh's life, and Lorna and her daughter flew in to attend his celebration of life. They were such a blessing—they bought everything that we needed. My sister's daughter even found a bouquet of flowers in a glass Mustang vase, and I still have it. They helped put the memory table of Josh together. It was beautiful that the pastor who baptized Josh in Missouri in 2004 flew in and did his celebration of life. On his flight down here with his friend, they were sitting by a young woman on the plane, talking to her about God. She listened to them and received her salvation. The church people fixed everybody a nice meal, and I am so thankful to everybody who helped us during our time of loss.

My daughter and I have been going through a lot of healing together. Since Josh passed away, we have continued going to the healing place that we had been going to for a while. They have a class going on there now where they bring in heaven and Jesus. It's called encounter prayer, and during that prayer time, Jesus gave my daughter a vision of my son and Jesus and angels around a campfire on the beach. Jesus brought Josh to my daughter and let her say the things she wanted to say to him, so she was able to tell him that she loved him and missed him and she was able to have closure with him.

Josh always wanted to be an actor or have something to do with the movie industry. He had the opportunity to go to acting school, and he did one commercial but was never able to go on and make a career of it. God gave Lorna a vision of Josh in heaven, writing movie scripts. God says:

> In the last days, I will pour my spirit on every kind of people Your sons will prophesy also your daughters Your young men will see visions your old men dream dreams when the time comes I'll pour out my spirit On those who serve me; men and women both and they'll prophesy. (Acts 2:17)

I kept my son's phone number that I had in my phone so I could keep the text messages; that he left me. My granddaughter thought that she could text Josh in heaven. So she text him a message. I was not aware that she had done that until one day I was checking my messages when I ran across this text that she had typed to him. "I love you Josh I know you're in heaven but can you answer this one text; what is God like? Is he funny?" An unknown person who had his number responded to the text and answered yes. When she seen the message she thought that it was Josh answering her, so she text back to him saying this message: Josh is that you? So you still text. I think you should talk to grandma. She misses you so much. Can you maybe show up as an angel and say hi or something? She would enjoy that."

God answered my granddaughter's request a couple months later through a prayer partner who I prayed with often. God let her hear Josh's voice to give me a message. This is what he said to her: "Hey, will you give my mom a message?" Even though the prayer partner had never met him or heard his voice, she knew at that moment who he was, and she answered, "Yes I sure will." Josh was talking real fast like he was on purpose going somewhere fast. My prayer partner told me he said, "Tell her I got in the school and taking classes for learning how to direct movies. First I have to finish all my classes and I have to help others produce a couple of movies. Then I get to direct my own movie, and accomplished actors already said they would be in it. Tell my mom by the time she gets here, it will be ready for everyone to watch."

I am so happy that Josh is living his dream in heaven. My daughter and I have been going to a recovery class at the church that we attend. The man who is leading the class is so anointed that on the first day I went there, he gave me these scriptures: Isaiah 57:1–2. It says:

> The righteous perish; and no one takes it to heart;
> the devout are taken away; and no one understands
> that the righteous are taken away to spare from evil.
> Those who walk uprightly enter into peace; they
> find rest as they lie in death.

Those scriptures have comforted me so much. I hope whoever is reading this book will find comfort in these scriptures. I include them here to share the comfort they have given me with anyone who has ever lost a loved one or loved ones before their time.

Our Journey and Healing

My son was thirty-eight years old when he passed away. Josh was my baby boy. He was born on October 31, 1979. It was Halloween when he came into this world. He loved life and his family very much. He was the comedian of the family. Although he struggled in this life, he made the most out of it. He loved the outdoors, and he loved music. He would sit on his porch in the early morning, watching the sun come up while listening to his music. He loved to sing and would rap to his favorite songs. He was very talented. He loved writing poems. He made weird faces and cracked jokes and could make anybody laugh.

Josh liked to impersonate the actor Jim Carrey. He was funny and acted just exactly like him. He even had his facial expressions and body language when he impersonated him. Josh was a very giving person. He wanted to help everybody, especially his family. He always had our backs. He stayed in contact with me. Often, he would call me on the phone to see how I was doing when I was sick. When my caretaker had to go out of town, Josh flew in from where he lived, cooked for me, and took care of me. I will never forget that he was a mama's boy and proud of it. He was a unique person that all of us will love and miss.

Josh had to be cremated. I thought that I would keep his ashes, but the people at the healing place that my family and I go to helped me to realize that it would be better if I set them free. Lorna flew down from Oregon to go to the healing place with me in August. Our appointments were on the tenth and eleventh.

When we went to our appointments on the tenth, they told me that I needed to let his ashes go. They had something come up on the eleventh, so they couldn't see us that day, and I decided to let Josh ashes go that day on the eleventh. It's amazing to me how all that turned out the way it did. I know that God was right there with us, hand-in-hand.

Josh liked the outdoors, and he liked fishing and camping, so we decided to let his ashes go by one of the lakes where we live. I wanted to have a song playing while we let his ashes go. I asked the Holy Spirit what would be a good song to play. That morning, Lorna's daughter texted her the song "Different" by Micah Tyler, so that's the song that we played. Lorna, my daughter, granddaughter, grandson, and I were all there when we set his ashes free. That song was the right choice because we were all going through healing.

We were all trying in our lives, to be different. We serve a loving God who is always with us, especially when we're going through hard things. After going through these things with Josh and saying goodbye to him, I was having a hard time dealing with who had done this to my son, feeling anger toward them and wanting them to pay for what they had done. One night, God woke me up and told me I needed to forgive the people who had murdered my son, so I did. By doing that, God set me free to go forward with my life. The first step to healing is the hardest step—to forgive the ones who hurt and abandon us and abuse us in such brutal ways—but it's the true beginning of total freedom, of forgiveness, that truly sets us free with God.

In light of our new beginnings, God commands that in return, we forgive others and extend grace as we have been shown grace. It can be one of the hardest things we face in life because the pain and hurt others cause us is real and great, but the pain of living with unforgiving and bitterness can poison your soul and destroy you. When we forgive others, we are not saying what they did was okay; we are releasing them to God and letting go of their hold on us. "For if you forgive other people when they sin against you your heavenly Father will also forgive you. But if you do not forgive others their sins your Father will not forgive your sins" (Matt. 6: 14–15). "Peter came to Jesus and asked Lord how many times shall I forgive my brother who sins against me? Up to seven times Jesus answered I tell you not seven times but seventy-seven times" (Matt. 18:21–22).

All things are possible. I have seen God throughout my life when things were not easy. Writing this book has made me realize that He has been with me all along. Through the good times and bad, He is with us no matter what we are facing. Losing my son is the hardest thing I have ever been through. It's been two and half years since my son went to heaven to be with Jesus. God has given me so many signs and wonders to know that He is here with me.

The months of May, June, July, and August have been the hardest for me. Josh passed on to be with Jesus in May, but his body wasn't found until June. In July, we had a celebration of life, and August was when we let his ashes go. It was the weekend of Mother's Day when he left his home, never to return. He would always call me or send me something in the mail. He wasn't able to do that the year that he left his home. This year 2020; on Mother's Day weekend, I had a strong feeling to go look around Hobby Lobby, so my granddaughter and I went shopping there. She went to look for something she wanted, so I went and looked down some of the aisles in the store. I had a strong feeling to look down this one aisle, and there I found this picture that had lettering that said, "If You Could See Me Now." It talks about what it's like to be in heaven. I knew God led me to that picture to let me know what Josh wanted to say to me. I was so overjoyed with excitement, knowing God loves me so much to give me comfort on Mother's Day by letting me know that my son is alive and happy with Him.

We attend a church where the pastor is a prominent pastor. My husband and granddaughter went to church; the pastor told everyone that they needed to give up something that they really liked because he was going to anoint the whole church. That Sunday, when they got home, they told me about it and wanted me to go with them the following Sunday. So we all gave up something that we liked so that we could receive the anointing that God wanted to give us. When the people began to move forward to receive the anointing; they went by the scripture in Matthew

20:16 where it says the last shall be first and the first last. It was so exciting to see everyone going forward to get anointed. We were all being set free from the yoke that enemy had us under; that affected all of our lives. God set us free from all the bondages in our finances, restoration in our bloodlines, and healing of broken hearts everywhere that had us bound up. After getting anointed, all that day we all felt calm and at peace.

On July 19, 2020, we went to church, and the sermon the pastor gave was on miracles and how they can happen in your life. We had recently moved, but before we moved into the house, my husband was there, and as he was leaving, he saw a beautiful rainbow over the house. That day, after getting home from church, my granddaughter was sitting on the couch watching television and playing on my phone. She said she felt something nudge her; to look out the window; she shouted out "Wow, wow, wow at that moment she experienced a sign and wonder!"— She saw an angel. The angel was in the same place where my husband had seen the rainbow. She had my phone in her hand and was able to take a picture of the angel. God has blessed us so much going through this time of 2020. He provided for us to gain financially and we accelerated in our faith together and we experienced rest and peace daily.

Angel

Soon after all this happened, I was listening to Christian music on the television, not knowing what songs would come up next. I was sitting on the couch with my phone, and the next song that came on was " If You Can See Me Now." I thought while I was listening to the song, I would paint a picture on Bible coloring on my phone. You don't know what the picture is going to be when you open it up, so when I opened it up, it said I love you. I felt so loved knowing how much my son loves me. God shows up in places that we don't expect, comforting us when we go through the loss of a loved one. Losing a child is like losing yourself as a mom. God has given me great signs and wonders and comfort, knowing that I will see my son again in heaven where he is living out his dreams and his destiny with God, Jesus and Holy Spirit.

Conclusion

Everything I went through in my past—a lot of trauma and pain—has affected my stomach. It has also affected the way I feel about myself, my self-image, never feeling good enough. The enemy puts all those thoughts that aren't true in your mind.

I know that throughout everything I have gone through with my healing that God, Jesus, and the Holy Spirit have been with me all along. God has helped and guided me to the right doctors and nutritionists that He wanted me to see, and also He provided me with the spiritual help I needed.

Throughout the years, the many prayer partners he brought into my life have given me hope, faith, and inspiration in God, Jesus, and the Holy Spirit, with the words that they have given to me. I have a lot of encouraging words that I have received throughout the years, so I can go back and read them when I get discouraged, and I can be built up, They remind me of everything I have been through with God, Jesus, and the Holy Spirit and how much they love me and how I can go to them in prayer with anything I have bothering me. I know that they are hearing me and will always help me with whatever I need or ask for, and I never give up.

Be still and know that He is God, and He is the same yesterday, today, and forever. Trust Him and have faith; He can make breakthroughs for anyone who calls upon His name. I have seen real breakthroughs happen in my life that have led me forward, and He has led Lorna and I to people who do what they have done for my future and for Lorna's. Throughout the years we have gone thru a lot of healing from our abusive past, and we are still getting healed. It's almost been a lifetime—our healing has been a journey, and God is not finished with us yet.

CPSIA information can be obtained
at www.ICGtesting.com
Printed in the USA
LVHW020100270721
693716LV00011B/370